COLOR

GOD'S INTENTION FOR DIVERSITY

CARLA D. SUNBERG
DANIEL A. K. L. GOMIS

THE FOUNDRY
PUBLISHING·

To God the Father, from whom every family in heaven and on earth derives its name.

To my father, Gabriel Jacques Gomis. I'm thankful for his legacy of open-mindedness, hospitality to every culture, and love for music and a simple life.

—Dany

To Frau Katarina Kühne, my German/Russian grandmother, who loved me and prayed over me, opening my ears and mind to the beauty of varied cultures.

—Carla

Cover Design: Arthur Cherry
Interior design by Michael J. Williams

Library of Congress Cataloging-in-Publication Data

Names: Sunberg, Carla D., author. | Gomis, Daniel A. K. L., 1969- author.
Title: Color : God's intention for diversity / Carla D. Sunberg, Daniel A.K.L. Gomis.
Description: Kansas City, MO : The Foundry Publishing, [2021] | Includes bibliographical references. | Summary: "The authors explore what it would look like for the Church to discover and use a full array of hues, both biblically and culturally, through reflections comparing a bride adorned in luxurious colors for her groom, to the bride of Christ"--Provided by publisher.
Identifiers: LCCN 2021000748 (print) | LCCN 2021000749 (ebook) | ISBN 9780834140356 (paperback) | ISBN 9780834140363 (ebook)
Subjects: LCSH: Christianity and culture. | Cultural pluralism--Religious aspects--Christianity.
Classification: LCC BR115.C8 S86 2021 (print) | LCC BR115.C8 (ebook) | DDC 270.089--dc23
LC record available at https://lccn.loc.gov/2021000748
LC ebook record available at https://lccn.loc.gov/2021000749

All Scripture quotations, unless indicated, are taken from THE HOLY BIBLE, NEW INTER-NATIONAL VERSION®, NIV® Copyright © 1973, 1978, 1984, 2011 by Biblica, Inc.® Used by permission. All rights reserved worldwide.

Scriptures marked (NRSV) are from the New Revised Standard Version Bible, copyright © 1989 the Division of Christian Education of the National Council of the Churches of Christ in the United States of America. Used by permission. All rights reserved.

Scriptures marked (ESV) are from *The Holy Bible, English Standard Version* (esv), copyright © 2001 by Crossway Bibles, a division of Good News Publishers. Used by permission. All rights reserved.

The internet addresses, email addresses, and phone numbers in this book are accurate at the time of publication. They are provided as a resource. The Foundry Publishing does not endorse them or vouch for their content or permanence.

10 9 8 7 6 5 4 3 2

CONTENTS

INTRODUCTION

"The princess is decked in her chamber with gold-woven robes; in many-colored robes she is led to the king; behind her the virgins, her companions, follow. With joy and gladness they are led along as they enter the palace of the king."

—Psalm 45:13b–15, NRSV

The psalmist paints the picture of a beautiful bride adorned for her bridegroom. One can only begin to imagine the splendor of the robes that are woven through with golden threads gleaming in the sun-drenched chambers. Her bearing is dignified, and she is draped in her many-colored garments before being led to the king. The magnitude of the honor the bride is given is reflected in the way in which she is now dressed and ready to enter the king's palace.

The vision of the bride was but a foreshadowing of the messianic era when the church would be birthed. The church—the bride of Christ—is to be ushered into the presence of the Bridegroom. Prepared for that day, the church will be adorned in beautiful many-colored robes, woven together with threads of gold, with design far outshining any human embroidery. The tapestry of these robes will come from the diversity of her people who are not mixed together to become uniform, but who are woven together by golden threads of faith and doctrine, creating a pattern so stunning that the world is left in awe.

Throughout her history the church has not always succeeded at reflecting such diversity. Far too often a desire for uniformity, or conformity, has prevailed. Sadly, this can paint a rather dull picture, one that can hardly compare with what God has intended. The only way the church can reflect the beauty that God planned is for brothers and sisters to come together in fellowship and conversation, allowing the Holy Spirit to weave them together into a divine reflection of the kingdom of God. This is our vision and dream for the church.

We are Dany and Carla, a brother and sister in Christ who have been spending time in conversation and fellowship. We are quite the unlikely pair to be writing a book together: Carla is a white woman who has lived twenty-one years of her life in Europe and speaks German, English, and Russian, while Dany is a black man who has lived most of his life in Senegal and speaks Wolof, French, and English. Through our work in the church, we were both thrust into brand-new positions that made us working partners for two years. During that time we, along with our spouses and other team members, spent a great deal of time traveling the continent of Africa, preaching, teaching, and fellowshipping. We all discovered that we had much to learn about the work we were doing, but also, about how we could work together, even when coming from such different backgrounds.

This book began as conversations around dinner tables where we would reflect upon what we had learned throughout the day. Honesty and trust opened the door for critical evaluation and continual improvement. Dany would share the things about Carla's messages that he liked and how it may relate to African culture, but he didn't hesitate to let her know when he thought she was off base. He would take the time to teach her deep underlying truths that affect the ways Africans would see and understand God. Carla would share with Dany about the theological truths he was embarking upon, and how they could be expanded when he allowed other voices to speak to him. She would talk to Dany about the ways he used music to communicate and relate to the people, often transforming a tense moment into one filled with the presence of God. This use of culture was a way God could be revealed to the people. They also had conversations about cultural misunderstandings and the realization that perceptions can be wrong.

The point is that we spent time talking and learning from one another, and we thought you might like to join us in these conversations. We discovered that when we allowed God to weave our work together, it was better and more beautiful than when we did it alone. We began to discover the beauty of the coat of many colors. Our brown and white became mixed with the incredible cultures we encountered. This is an invitation for you to join our personal journeys, and then our combined work as disciples who are processing this Christian walk.

We are living in a world that is changing at a rapid pace, and the experiences along the way helped to shape our conversations. When reflecting upon the past we recognize that at times the church has lived with an "us and them" mentality, and as much as we would like to shake that off, it's been a struggle. We might think that this is in regard to our missional enterprise, but it may also be an attitude of one culture viewing itself as dominant, and usually entering other cultures as a host rather than a guest.

Christian hospitality lies at the foundation of a relationship of mutuality and, depending upon the situation, the role of guest and host shifts.

In reality, the church is not much different from the rest of the world, which still believes there is dichotomy: That some are always the hosts, and others are always the guests. Sometimes we have embraced the mindset and language of a "developed" and a "developing world." For others, it may simply be a dichotomy between your cultural worldview and another person's.

Many of us have remained frozen in a 1960s picture of the world, and the church. Dr. Hans Rosling, in his book *Factfulness*, shatters the 1960s notions of the world, encouraging us to see that we have come a long way since then, and along with the changes in the world have come major implications for the church. When we examine the world, we discover there is no longer any economic dichotomy of "us" and "them," rather Dr. Rosling places the world on four levels of economic development. The number living in level one (the poorest) continues to decrease at a dramatic pace, while those on level four, coming from outside the "Northern Hemisphere and the West" will soon overtake those who had retained single occupancy in that category. In other words, the economic development in the world is happening rapidly, and this has implications for all of God's people. The one who was assumed to always be the guest, rightfully, plays the role of host.

We can rejoice that these changes have occurred, and the church has been a very active participant in bringing change in many parts of the world. Without the work of missionaries and Christian humanitarian agencies, and the resilience and contribution of national Christian leadership, much of this progress may not have occurred. The exciting news is that many throughout the world have been lifted economically, socially, and educationally and are now ready to take their rightful place in leadership. This can be a challenge because we must work to intentionally break away from the old ways. This is an exciting time to be a part of the church, for we get to lean into a new future, one that has never before been explored or experienced, but that is only possible when we are willing to intentionally work at change.

This book is an endeavor to bring together radically different cultures, revealing a coat of many colors, which, in its beauty, reflects the kingdom of God. Doctrine is a golden thread that helps in weaving us together. The message of holiness transcends culture and calls us to be united. This work is not easy, but it is a labor of love for the church so that the bride may be resplendent with beauty.

QUESTIONS FOR REFLECTION

1. Why are you interested in embarking on this conversation about diversity in the church?

_____

_____

_____

2. What are your thoughts on multicultural churches and a focus on monocultural churches of one ethnicity?

_____

_____

_____

3. What changes have you seen in the last ten to twenty years that may have shaped your thinking about the future of the church?

_____

_____

_____

1

BROWN

Dany's Story

Words. Words help us to categorize and classify in order to better identify, study, explore, and understand. Words are used to express an idea, an idea that becomes a picture, a picture that may become a stereotype, and a stereotype turns into an object, a fact, then finally a truth and a story. Words are powerful, indeed, but pictures are often more impactful.

As a child, I grew up with two pictures of Jesus: baby Jesus and the crucified Jesus. In my little mind, Jesus was depending totally upon his mother, Mary, and I had to make my prayer requests to her. I came from a divorced family where my brothers and sisters were separated at a young age and sent to different homes. I lived with my father, and a deep sense of insecurity grew within me. I could not put my trust in a baby Jesus who was depending on his mother. The other picture was of the crucified Jesus, nailed on a cross, half naked, with eyes closed as if defeated, his head leaning to the right side and looking down. His mother was sitting at the foot of that cross, watching and crying. This also did not speak very much to me in those early years of my life.

As a young child, I did not notice Jesus's skin color because what I saw must have been normal. Jesus could not have been anything other than . . . white. My religious representation of God was white, because our Catholic priest, Father Lebert, who was an old Frenchman, taught us catechism and was assisted by white French nuns. Very few nuns were Senegalese. When I celebrated my Catholic communion, I was so proud to wear my white shirt with my cardigan, blue velvet pants, and a red bowtie, while my friends stood next to me with their white suits or dresses. I still have our Catholic confirmation picture in which my sister Stephanie and I are wearing white albs, with huge wooden crosses around our necks, belts made of wool on our waists. Our hands are joined, and we have smiles on our faces. It was one of my closest experiences of looking like Father Lebert.

I was studying in the French language, learning about the French culture, and the heroes in all of my cartoon books were white. I admired Zembla—one of those heroes—a herculean white man with long black hair who lived in the jungle of Africa. He could speak with the wild animals and was fighting for the local African tribes against cruel tribal chiefs and greedy white traders.

I also loved Antares, a blond, handsome, and powerful superhero who could live both under the sea and on the earth and could speak with all the animals in the ocean. The amazing thing in my young child's imagination was to see him having a dolphin as his horse. Tex Willer was one my favorite heroes. Tex was a U.S. ranger who defended Native Americans from the exaction and greed of bandits, unscrupulous merchants, and corrupt politicians and tycoons.

Throughout my entire childhood, most of my heroes were white males, who had a strong sense of justice, could live in any cultural or social context, all the while bringing about change and hope. My heroes were Father Lebert, Zembla, or Tex Willer. My world as an African boy, living on African soil, was populated with a white world. Both my religious and fantasy worlds were white, and in those days, I didn't question any of it. All of this had become normal, because as Frantz Fanon ironically said, "For the black man there is only one destiny. And it is white."[1]

I was not aware that I lived with a particular narrative that had been with me from my childhood until I started to listen to reggae music in my teenage years. I also began to read new authors while in high school and added even more while attending public university. In reality, the turning point came when my father died. I was only nineteen, but my father had suffered through a long illness. My world collapsed, and my hope for a bright future became very dim. I found myself in a profound crisis of identity. My father had been Roman Catholic, but I realized that I had never really fit into the religion. I did not sense any connection with the two pictures of Jesus from my childhood: baby Jesus and Jesus on the cross. Suddenly I became aware that both of these versions of Jesus, his mother, all the angels, and even God, were white. I did not feel comfortable in their company because I did not belong. I needed spirituality more in line with my African culture, more in tune with my day-to-day experience, and I was desperately in search of a spiritual mentor with whom I could identify.

1. Frantz Fanon, *Black Skin, White Masks* (New York: Grove Press, 1967).

From my teens to my mid-twenties, I surrounded myself with mentors who shaped my thinking. I found these mentors in books and music, people like Bob Marley, Steve Biko, Frantz Fanon, Malcolm X, and many others.

I consciously decided to reject anything related to European Christianity and the cultural values that were part of my inherited identity. I became more and more interested in African languages, history, and culture, and as I could not separate Christianity from its Eurocentric approach, I decided to convert into Islam. Not just any kind of Islam, but an African version of Islam.

I needed a spiritual mentor, and I could not find one in the totally white Christianity of my childhood. I turned to Islam but was not interested in Muhammad, the Prophet of Islam, because he also was a white Arab. However, my spiritual thirst was for a personal relationship with a spiritual guide. This was not a religious, formal, or legalistic type of guide, but I sought a mystical, simple, deep, and authentic relationship that would be in sync with my African identity. I became interested in the Muridiyya Sufi movement in Islam and the teachings of Sheikh Ahmadou Bamba, its Senegalese religious founder. I discovered a sense of community, of belonging, and a way to develop a mystical relationship. However, as I was on that journey, a major defining spiritual experience would completely change the trajectory of my life.

One day, while reading the Quran, a verse[2] on Jesus the Messiah triggered questions[3] in my mind, and I started a quest

2. Surah 3:55: "When Allah said, 'O Jesus, indeed *I will take you and raise you to Myself and purify you from those who disbelieve* and **make those who follow you superior to those who disbelieve until** the Day of Resurrection. Then to Me is your return, and I will judge between you concerning that in which you used to differ'" (emphases added).

3. As I was reading the Quran in order to find arguments so that I could refute the divinity of Jesus, the concept of the Trinity, and the crucifixion of Jesus, this verse stood

to know more about him. I was in my mid-twenties when I started reading the Gospels for the first time with a new desire, to understand more about Jesus. I met Jesus as a real person who invited me to walk alongside him on a pilgrimage of self-discovery. It was an invitation into a very intimate and open relationship that would include candid and honest conversations about my fears, my internal struggles, my insecurities, and my African identity. Eventually I could join Job in saying, "My ears had heard of you but now my eyes have seen you" (Job 42:5).

From my childhood to my mid-twenties, I had been like Zacchaeus, watching Jesus from afar, hearing about his story from well-intentioned people but who had dressed him in their own cultural biases, and taught me through the eyes of his mother with an emphasis on a spirituality of poverty, submission, dependence, and resignation. Now, my eyes had seen him, and as a proverb in my language says: "You cannot deny what you see with your own eyes."

I plunged into the stories in all four of the Gospels. The next thing I knew, I was imagining myself walking next to Jesus, listening to his teachings, and taking note of his gestures and responses to the people from every walk of life who had come to see him. No longer was I seeing a picture on the wall of a baby Jesus or a crucifix of Jesus in a house, but I was meeting a person, a real man, who lived and walked on earth and spoke simply, and in everyday language about the deepest spiritual and timeless truths I had ever heard. I did not see the white Jesus represented in my childhood pictures, but I saw a Jewish

---

out as it stated that those who follow Jesus (not those who believed in him, because Muslims claim to believe in Jesus but they follow Muhammad, the Prophet of Islam) will be above those who don't believe in Jesus. I also discovered that the Quran was quoting Jesus more than the Prophet of Islam himself—in his own book—and the only chapter in the Quran with the name of a woman was named after Mary the mother of Jesus.

man who lived in the Middle East, who was born under colonial rule, who spent the early formative years of his life as a refugee in Africa (Matthew 2:13), who ate while sitting on the floor using his hands, and who was always in community.

Beyond the common cultural connections that I saw in him because of his Jewish culture and habits, I also connected with his universal message of hope, reconciliation, and love. I later realized that even during the wildest years of my university studies, while I was proudly displaying the Rastafarian philosophy outwardly, and inwardly adopting an African type of Islam, I had written the three answers Jesus gave to the devil when he was tempted in the wilderness, on the door of the closet in my dorm room.[4] It was as if something in me knew that Jesus Christ was to become the answer to my quest.

And yes, it is a quest, a discovery, and a relationship with Jesus who discloses himself to us as our relationship goes deeper and deeper. Didn't he say in John 8:32: "You will know the truth, and the truth will set you free"? He did not say that the truth has set me free, or sets me free but rather it "will." The freedom or liberation process has happened indeed, is currently happening, and will continue to happen. The Lord Jesus knew that I still had a few more struggles to deal with in my inner life. Remember, I had grown up with a picture of Jesus as a baby who depended on his mother and a defeated man on a cross. These images were a major obstacle in my search for a spiritual mentor, for I was a young man who had lost his father and needed a real man in his life. I must confess that, in my eyes, Jesus was not manly enough.

A key discovery for me came when I saw the manhood of Jesus masterfully described by J. Oswald Sanders in *The*

---

4. Matthew 4:4: "It is written: 'Man shall not live on bread alone, but on every word that comes from the mouth of God.'" Matthew 4:7: "Do not put the Lord your God to the test." Matthew 4:10: "Worship the Lord your God, and serve him only."

Incomparable Christ.[5] I was desperately seeking a spiritual mentor, and the chapter on "the manliness of Christ" spoke to my need. Sanders opens with these words, "Jesus was not only a man, He was a manly man—the crown and glory of humanity."[6] Sanders described his resolute courage, his intrepid utterances, his physical endurance, his courageous silence, his unbending sternness, his remarkable self-control, his blistering denunciations, and his uncompromising frankness. Just like Sanders, I find much inspiration in Rex Boundy's poem:

> Give us a virile Christ for these rough days!
> You painters, sculptors, show the warrior bold;
> And you who turn mere words to gleaming gold,
> Too long your lips have sounded in the praise
> Of patience and humility. Our ways have parted
> From the quietude of old;
> We need a man of strength with us to hold
> The very breach of death without amaze.
> Did He not scourge from temple courts the thieves?
> And make the archfiend's self again to fall?
> And blast the fig tree that was only leaves?
> And still the raging tumult of the seas?
> Did He not bear the greatest pain of all,
> Silent upon the Cross on Calvary?[7]

I began my spiritual journey with Jesus as guide, and he transformed my distorted vision of God, my disturbed and deranged vision of myself, and my biased vision of the other. This journey is usually called discipleship or the process of sanctification. I see it as a rehearsal for a better and everlasting

---

5. J. Oswald Sanders, *The Incomparable Christ* (Chicago: Moody Publishers, 1952), 69.
6. Sanders, *Incomparable*, 69.
7. Sanders, *Incomparable*, 117–18.

life, but a life lived in the current reality. I believe that God was reaching out to me from a young age and even through my culture. I began to have a vision of God through the everyday experiences of life. When I was a little boy, I loved the rain, and every time there was lightning, I used to say that God was taking a picture of us! God had always been part of our worldview, and we never questioned nor doubted his existence. We called him *Maam Yallà,* which meant "Grandfather God," and at each rainy season we sang a song: *Grandfather God give me water and if I live, I will pay you your water back."* We would sing it and sing it again until it rained. And when it rained, we would run out into the raindrops, jump in the muddy streets, and shout for joy with gratitude. In our innocent minds, we were convinced that *Maam Yallà* heard our prayers and was sending us the lightning to have a picture of us that he would keep in his home. *Maam Yallà* was far in the sky but he was near. Every day we would mention him in all that we did, and we expected him to be part of our lives because he was our Grandfather God. *Maam Yallà* and *Jamm* (peace) were mentioned in our greetings, before and after our meals, before traveling, and in our blessings. *Maam Yallà* was an extension of our family, an integral part of our daily activities, and he was shared with my childhood friend Paap and many others who were Muslims. It did not make any difference; when we were jumping and shouting and singing under the rain, we were all speaking to the same Grandfather, *Maam Yallà.*

Jamm, or peace, binds every aspect or area of our worldview, our cosmic view, and our social interactions. Everything must be done to preserve peace for the sake of harmony between the visible and invisible worlds, which were interacting and never viewed as separate or distinct. Just as *Maam Yallà* was everywhere and in everything we did, we also believed good and bad spirits mingled in our earthly lives and in the cosmic world.

Songs, music, and dancing were natural parts of our growing up, and this all began when a baby was tied on the back of her mother, who sang while doing chores. It was an integrated world in which superstitions and taboos were used to forbid the young from doing dangerous things but also to awaken their curiosity and creativity.

One day, I started to attend catechism classes at our local, small, Roman Catholic chapel and was introduced to "Le Bon Dieu" ("The Good God" in French). He spoke another language, and I learned about him in a classroom taught by French priests who were the intermediaries between him and us. The *Bon Dieu* was organized, structured, untouchable, and unreachable, and was to be addressed in French or, even better, in Latin. He was to be studied in a picture book. *Maam Yallà* was everywhere, and I could speak to him in my own language about all my little troubles and issues; he was in the cosmic world, but he was also with me on the playground with my friends.

I lived in tension between the *Bon Dieu* and *Maam Yallà* even after I became a follower of Jesus Christ. The songs, the prayers, and the teachings in the *Bon Dieu* perspective were very heavenly, focused on highly spiritual issues and expressed in systematic and descriptive ways. For example, when Jesus said, "Blessed are the poor in spirit," it was explained as an encouragement to live in physical poverty in order to have spiritual richness. Without our realizing it, a mentality of poverty was being developed in many of our minds, and simplicity in dress and appearance was seen as one of the most important aspects of this poverty. When Jesus said, "Blessed are those who hunger and thirst for righteousness," it was seen more as living in piety, in submission, and obedience than a desire to seek social justice in a context where many are oppressed and living with injustices.

The lyrics of the worship songs were foreign to me. Songs like: "You can hate me, reject me, curse me here on earth. It does not matter; my homeland is in heaven. I will go there," or "White as snow; washed in the blood of Jesus, I will be as white as snow." These two songs are examples of a theology made of escapism and of contextual irrelevance. I came to realize the last song was not comprehendible when I was singing one day in Ouagadougou, Burkina Faso, in the heart of the Sahel, where the temperature can go up to 45 degrees Celsius (120F) and where no one singing that day had ever seen snow! The *Bon Dieu* was getting further and further away from our daily routine, our experiences, and life.

In several instances, I felt like the Syrophoenician woman who was willing to take the crumbs falling from the master's table (Matthew 15:21-28). I realized that I had the wrong approach; in fact, the *Bon Dieu* was a cultural construct developed for a specific mindset, and I had to look at it as one of the seats at the table rather than consider that this was the table itself. For years, I behaved like young David when he met King Saul and told him he would defeat Goliath. At that moment the king gave him, in fact he lent him, his armor: "Then Saul dressed David in his own tunic. He put a coat of armor on him and a bronze helmet on his head. David fastened on his sword over the tunic and tried walking around, because he was not used to them" (1 Samuel 17:38–39*a*).

David receiving borrowed armor and trying to move without success is a picture of my struggle in wearing a vision of God that could not fit me, because it was not made for me. Unlike David—who was authentic and courageous enough to say to the king: "'I cannot go in these,' he said to Saul, 'because I am not used to them.' So he took them off. Then he took his staff in his hand, chose five smooth stones from the stream, and put them in the pouch of his shepherd's bag and, with his sling in his hand, approached the Philistine" (1 Samuel 17:39*b*-40)—I tried for years to wear someone else's armor until I came to realize, just as the Cameroonian theologian Jean-Marc Ela said, "Nothing was obliging me to stand before God wearing a *borrowed humanity*."[8]

From my teenage years to the day Jesus encountered me sitting alone in my university dorm room, I was longing for freedom. For me, this meant that I had to come to God as I am, in my own uniqueness, my own cultural background, and my own self. I had to put aside any borrowed humanity or interpretation of God. I had been looking for that freedom through different prisms and lenses, but then I came to know the Truth, and that Truth has set me free. In Jesus, and through faith in Jesus, I can now approach God *with freedom and confidence* (Ephesians 3:12) and sit at the table in the kingdom of God (Luke 13:29, ESV).

---

8. Jean-Marc Ela, *My Faith as an African* (Eugene, OR: Wipf and Stock Publishers, 1988).

QUESTIONS FOR REFLECTION

1. What are your first impressions of Jesus?

_____

_____

_____

2. Who was influential in your spiritual development?

_____

_____

_____

3. What do you think about the possibility of God using the Quran to lead someone to Christ? What does this teach us about grace?

_____

_____

_____

4. Thinking about your own culture, what is it that has taught you about God?

_____

_____

_____

2

WHITE

Carla's Story

The global north. You can't be much whiter or European than I am. My childhood provided me with rich experiences that helped to shape and form my ideas about God. Growing up in the city of Frankfurt, Germany, I found that almost every day was an experience that filled my senses with the history of Christianity. Sometimes I tell people that I think Germany invented Christmas—or at least many of the traditions that the Western or Protestant churches follow. The Christmas market would fill the downtown of the city, a place that had been known as the heart of the Free Imperial City of Frankfurt, a major city of the Holy Roman Empire. The sites of the Römerplatz and the Frankfurt Cathedral, decorated for the holiday season, remain in my memory, and even now I can smell the evergreens.

While the city itself was magical during the Christmas season, the traditions made their way to our home where we celebrated Advent for the entire month of December. We always had an Advent calendar with little windows that were opened daily, as well as a wreath on which we lit the candle every Sunday. All of this was in anticipation of the arrival of the Christ child on Christmas Eve. We would go to church where we received a red candle with a sprig of evergreen, held together by plaster of paris. The songs of Christmas filled the air as the room was lit by candlelight. The evening always ended with the singing of "*Stille Nacht* (Silent Night)." I didn't really comprehend the significance at the time, but my child's heart was warmed as I imagined the arrival of a little baby who was swaddled and laid in a manger. This was the Jesus of my childhood: sweet, tender, and innocent.

Not everything in my childhood was that innocent, and there were moments of genuine fear. I was born the summer that the Berlin Wall began to rise, only a few hours' drive from where we lived. I attended a United States Department of Defense (DOD) kindergarten and elementary school that were always under high levels of security. We were children from very diverse backgrounds who were brought together to study because of our citizenship. There was no segregation in these schools, and little did we know that there were issues back in the United States. We blissfully studied together, children of every color and background, enjoying our friendships. That peace was often disrupted by air-raid drills and even bomb threats, which would get us sent home for the day. My classmates' parents were sent off to other parts of the world, and the highways around our town had speed limits for tanks. The innocent and sweet Jesus from my early years didn't seem to be powerful enough to take away the terror at the thought of war. The bombed-out opera house in the heart of the city was a gaping wound and continual reminder that everything wasn't safe.

Throughout those early years, I saw glimpses of Jesus through different experiences. My mother became a reflection of Jesus for me because of the ways she responded to what was happening in the world. She seemed brave and capable while, at the same time, compassionate. One night as we were having supper, there was a knock at the front door. I must have been five or six years old, and I remember following Mom to the door to peek at who had come. Curiosity has always gotten the better of me, and after seeing the big man dressed in rags at the front door, Mom sent me back to the kitchen and to supper. She didn't say a word, but went to the cupboard and made a big sandwich, wrapped it in paper, and took it to the door. I knew that she had very little food to spare in the house, but she was generous with the poor man begging at our home. I looked at my mother in wonder, and caught a small glimpse of Jesus in action.

This wouldn't be the only time that my mother would shape my thinking about Jesus. My parents organized a camp meeting in Kaiserslautern near the big military base. They often ministered in German and in English with different congregations. Cooking for large groups was a skill my mother learned back on the Canadian farm where she was raised. She shared this gift with others as she organized the meals for those attending.

One night a man stumbled through the property where the camp meeting was being held. He was poorly dressed and his hands were wrapped in filthy rags. My parents greeted him and encouraged him to sit down and have supper with all of us. The man was shy and not sure that he should stay. He seemed embarrassed about his hands and my mother asked if she could take a look at them. Gently, she unwrapped the filthy dressings and found that both hands had terrible wounds. While caring for him, she discovered that he had been a German soldier during the war and had spent a great amount of time on the Russian front. He was reported missing, and then dead, by the authorities. He was gone for more than five years, and when he returned home after walking all the way from Russia, he ascertained that his wife had remarried and had a new family. He was homeless and had been wandering for years. Day after day, my mother cared for his wounds until he was healed. She told the man about the Jesus she loved, and he became a believer, eventually becoming the organist at the church that was planted in the town. The compassion of the Jesus my parents spoke of came to life in my mother's acts.

Sweet, tender, innocent, and compassionate—these are words that describe the Jesus of my early years, but there would be a traumatic event that would shake my faith to the core. Approaching my eighth birthday, I learned that we would be moving to the United States. I had visited there twice before, but the country seemed distant, foreign, and huge. Everything in America seemed different to me. I remember thinking that the houses all looked temporary, because they were made of wood. I lived in a city with buildings nearly one thousand years old, and nothing in America had been around that long!

We were not able to take much with us when we left, and I remember my old dollhouse being taken from me and set outside. Some neighbor boys came by and tore it to pieces, and I cried. The day we left I put on my little green overcoat and held my doll in a vise-grip. At the airport our dear German friends came and sang "*Gott Sei Mitt Euch* (God Be with You 'til We Meet Again)," and I felt like my heart was ripping out of my chest. How could God ask me to leave everything that I loved so fiercely? Suddenly Jesus no longer seemed sweet, tender, innocent, and compassionate, and fear would become glued to my heart to be my new companion.

We arrived in the Bay Area of California in the summer of 1969. The culture shock couldn't have been much more radical as we encountered this strange new world. People were friendly and spoke English, but I didn't always understand what they meant by the words they spoke, and I certainly didn't know how to fit in. My first day of school, I was petrified. I cried, trying to hold back the sobs as my parents left me to navigate this new environment. The children made fun of my Canadian accent (I'd learned to speak English from my mother), and laughed at the hand-crocheted sweater I wore. The food in my lunchbox was healthy but looked foreign compared to the snack cakes and chips the others had. Pictures of Jesus were pushed from my mind as I tried to cope with a whole new world, wondering how I would fit in.

Christmas came, and the Jesus who was a part of my childhood became more of a distant memory. Someone from the church thought they would help us with our culture shock, so they brought us a "flocked" Christmas tree. It had fake snow on it and did nothing to remind us of home. The traditions were gone, there was no Christmas market, and it was hot outside.

After only thirteen months, my father was called to a church in another state, Idaho, and the transition continued. Another first day of school. Another day of tears. Then, after two weeks I had to move to another school because of boundary changes, and the tears flooded again. A year later, an experiment with a sixth-grade school, and I had to move again. More tears. Seventh grade began at another school, and I thought I was holding it together until a month into the school year, my parents announced we were moving again, to Kansas City. And yes—more tears.

In all of my childhood education, I attended thirteen different schools, and fears inside of me continued to grow and the layers of protection around my heart became thicker. I went to church and did all the right things, not because I knew Jesus, but because I wanted to be accepted. Thoughts of Jesus were now distant.

Somehow, I'm always drawn back to my mother as the central figure in my spiritual development. I know she never gave up praying for me, or for any of her children. One summer, I headed off to teen camp with a group of my friends. Again, I was seeking to be accepted, trying to figure out how to fit in while my German life always seemed to hang onto me. I didn't catch the jokes, and didn't know the American TV shows. Our family didn't eat the same foods, or have holidays the way my American friends did. My mother sewed my clothes and I wanted store-bought, and all of this affected the way I saw Jesus. Why would he make me so odd? And there I was at camp, my hearing drowned out by the culture I wanted to accept me, when Jesus got my attention.

Again, it must have been my mother, because I don't have any idea what the preacher talked about that evening, but I felt drawn toward Jesus. This wasn't the Jesus of my childhood, but a Jesus who was reaching out to me in the midst of my teenage angst. I tried to run, leaving the tabernacle, and found a friend outside. We talked, and I told her that I thought I needed to go back and give my life to Jesus. That night, I wrestled with simply going through the motions of the religion I had been handed or getting to know Jesus in a personal way. Prevenient grace must have touched my heart, and I knew I needed to respond. Turning around, I made my way back into the sanctuary, opening my deeply protected heart to Jesus. That night changed my life and my ideas about Jesus.

There was so much about life in America that I still didn't understand. I would listen to the radio in Kansas City and hear about the murder rate. I was terrified and had trouble sleeping at night, convinced that someone would sneak into our house and murder my mom and me. In Germany we had large shutters that closed the windows at night, but in America, there was no covering.

By now, most of the time, my mother and I were the only two left at home, with my brothers either graduated or in college, and my father on the road for the church. I finally admitted to my mother that I couldn't sleep and that I was often afraid. She came into my room and read to me from Psalm 4:8, "In peace I will lie down and sleep, for you alone, LORD, make me dwell in safety." Suddenly, it was as if Jesus filled my room. When I had trouble sleeping at night, I would look over and Jesus was as real as someone sitting in the rocking chair watching over me. Gradually, my early impressions of the sweet, tender, innocent, and compassionate Jesus began to return.

It's interesting how so much of our understanding of Christ comes from the world in which we live. We all have different experiences and pathways through life, but somehow, God's prevenient grace is always present, drawing us toward a relationship of holy love with God and with the world. No matter who we are or what culture we come from, God is there. No single road to Christ is better than the other, for in God, we experience diversity. When we embrace the expressions of Christ that we have learned from our cultural and life experiences, we discover that we are invited to bring them to the table, where they can be distributed as a testimony to the beautiful diversity in the body of Christ. Therefore, I can't say to my German heritage, "I don't need you." Nor can I ignore my American life, for this helped to shape me. And finally, when I learned to speak Russian, a whole new image of Christ was opened to me through the richness of language.

In 1991, the church asked my husband and me to consider moving to Russia. For the little girl who was terrified of the Berlin Wall, this was quite a stretch, but in the moment that we were asked to go, God's peace washed over me in an unexplainable way. God took away my fear and replaced it with love in a way that carried me through thirteen years of service in a place where I probably should have been afraid. Even when we heard gunshots outside and the constant echo of car alarms, I would put my head down and rest.

Russians often refer to their language as *bogatyy*, which means "rich." Just google the word "go" and it will provide you with sixty-nine different verbs that could mean "go" in the Russian language. It all depends on whether you're going on foot, by vehicle, beginning to go, intending to return, going and coming regularly, just going and never coming back, etc. This language is not easy to learn, requiring years of study, but once it gets into your heart and mind, it opens up an understanding of Christ that takes on a new vibrancy of understanding.

This language should have been out of my reach, yet it seemed to find a home in my head. Little did I realize that this was a gift from God placed upon me from my infancy. The year I was born, my parents were busy starting a Bible college in Frankfurt. My mother was one of the first teachers in the program and had to find someone to care for me.

One of the first believers in the church in Germany was Frau Kühne, who had given her life to the Lord while at the dining room table with my mother. This dear lady became my German grandmother, caring for me in my infancy, but also throughout my childhood. Because my mother played the organ in church, all four of us children were distributed throughout the congregation with our German surrogate family members. Frau Kühne was known as Katushka to me, and she would hug me close in church and keep me quiet with good German chocolate every Sunday morning. This dear German grandmother even came to America to be my grandmother for my wedding!

When my husband, Chuck, and I were on our way to Russia, we stopped in Germany to visit Katushka. There, we sat and talked in German, reminiscing about my childhood years. Suddenly, she stopped and looked at me and said, "You know I'm not German, don't you?" I had always known in the back of my mind that she was Russian, but it didn't really register because she was my German grandma. She went on to say, "When you were a baby, I used to sing lullabies to you in Russian." Finally, she commented, "For thirty years I have prayed that my church would go behind the Iron Curtain and tell my family about Jesus. I never thought it would be the baby that I cared for who would go to Russia."

A short time later I was able to meet Magda Alexandrovna, Katushka's little sister who lived in Moscow, and tell her about Jesus. Just as my mother led Katushka to the Lord, I was able to pray with her sister at the kitchen table, in answer to a thirty-year-old prayer. I was able to learn to speak because my infant ears had been attuned to the beautiful and rich Russian language from the time of my birth.

Russia of the 1990s was often described as the Wild West. Life was chaotic as the newly independent nations created laws, economic standards, and infrastructure to support a new paradigm. From one day to the next, one lived with ambiguity, wondering if you may be stranded across a newly formed border, have your car confiscated, or find yourself deported for some new law. In the midst of this chaos, Russia helped me to know Christ in a deeper way.

There is an ancient Russian saying, "One has not seen beauty who has not seen Moscow." During the period of Pushkin, had you visited Moscow, you would have been overwhelmed with the beauty of the horizon covered with golden church domes gleaming in the sun. Beauty and Christianity were melded together in a vision almost too glorious to behold.

The word for the color red also has its roots in the word for beauty. Therefore, at the center of Moscow, one finds Red Square—not because it symbolizes communism but because the city had its roots in the beauty of participation with God. The gates of the Kremlin were Christian in name, from the Trinity Gate Tower to Annunciation Tower. Every week Russians have a Sabbath on Saturday and celebrate resurrection on Sunday since these are the literal words for those days of the week. This is a very rich language that provides for a unique expression of the beauty found in a relationship between God and humankind.

Russia introduced me to the early church fathers and volumes of their works produced in the Russian language. Here I began to learn about God's gracious invitation found in Peter's second epistle: "His divine power has given us everything needed for life and godliness, through the knowledge of him who called us by his own glory and goodness. Thus he has given us, through these things, his precious and very great promises, so that through them you may escape from the corruption that is in the world because of lust, and may become participants of the divine nature" (2 Peter 1:3–4, NRSV). This language of participation was intriguing to me as I discovered that Jesus provided a way for me to have intimate fellowship with the triune God. The more real that Christ became to me, the greater I desired to know him. Following and imitating Jesus has become the goal for my life.

Gregory of Nyssa, one of the church fathers, wrote *On Perfection*, which has been beautifully translated into English by my former professor at Nazarene Theological Seminary, Dr. Paul Bassett.[9] What we learn in his writing is that through the practice of virtue "we become an image of the image, having achieved the beauty of the Prototype [who is Christ] through activity as a kind of imitation, as did Paul, who became an 'imitator of Christ' [1 Corinthians 4:16] through his life of virtue."[10] In other words, the more time that we spend in intimate fellowship with God and imitating Christ, the more we become like him, and the result is a reflection of the Lord's beauty to the world.

Gregory of Nyssa continued this theme in his *Commentary on Song of Solomon* saying that "by coming closer to the inaccessible Beauty [Christ] you have yourself become beautiful, and like a mirror, as it were, you have taken on my appearance,"[11] meaning the beautiful appearance of the Bridegroom. "Hence the Word says to her: You have become fair because you have come near to my light, and by this closeness to me you have attracted this participation in beauty."[12] Participation in the beauty of Christ can, potentially, transform every aspect of life.[13]

As I read further in Nyssen's *Commentary*, I was drawn in by this understanding of participation in God's holy love. He wrote of the beautiful bride: "By a delicious wound she receives His special dart in her heart; and then she herself becomes the arrow in the hand of the Bowman, who with his right hand

9. See Paul M. Bassett, *Holiness Teaching: New Testament Times to Wesley.* Vol. 3 of *Great Holiness Classics* (Kansas City: Beacon Hill Press of Kansas City, 1997).

10. Nyssen, DP (GNO III.I) (FC, 111).

11. Nyssen, CC, Homily 4 (PG 44:832–33c) (GNO VI), trans. Musurillo, 171.

12. Nyssen, CC, Homily 4.

13. Carla D. Sunberg, *The Cappadocian Mothers: Deification Exemplified in the Writings of Basil, Gregory, and Gregory* (Eugene, OR: Pickwick Publications), 143.

draws the arrow near to himself, and with his left directs its head towards the heavenly goal."[14] The wounds of life that can be filled with divine love bring healing from the inside out. This is God's holy love that anoints the wounds. The wounds that resulted from the fears I had throughout life could now become open vessels, ready recipients of God's divine healing. "By being filled with the love of the bowman, [the bride's] head is now turned heavenward, and the focus of all her attention becomes the bridegroom. No longer is transformation the goal; he is the goal."[15]

My understanding of Christ was radically changed as I came to understand that the journey of life is one in which we can continually fall deeper in love with the Bridegroom. The desires and passions in life are to be for Jesus Christ, and him alone. I'm grateful for my Russian sisters and brothers who taught me to sing with all my heart, "Lublu Tebya" ("I love you, Lord"), for this reflects the richness and beauty of knowing Christ.

The entirety of this journey allows me to realize there is always something more just beyond my reach. When we are participating in life with an eternal God, there will always be more to learn and understand. That's the beauty of what happens when white meets brown.

14. Nyssen, *CC*, Homily 6 (PG 44:888c–893c) (GNO VI), trans. Musurillo, 198.
15. Sunberg, *Cappadocian*, 147–48.

QUESTIONS FOR REFLECTION

1. What childhood experiences shaped your understanding of Jesus?

_____

_____

_____

2. How did your perception of Jesus speak to your needs throughout life, and did it change from time to time?

_____

_____

_____

3. Who has represented Christ for you?

_____

_____

_____

4. How does the language or languages you speak influence your understanding of God?

_____

_____

_____

3

WHAT COLOR IS MY JESUS?

Carla

After spending months on the continent of Africa, I realized that my traditional notions about Christ were being challenged. I began to ask myself whether the Jesus I knew and loved was based upon my own social construct, and whether I was open to having those boundaries expanded.

As I mentioned before, I grew up in Germany where my parents were missionaries. We didn't have a lot of financial resources, but my mother always made sure we were well cared for, and that included looking nice. I didn't appreciate my mother's sewing skills at the time because I wanted store-bought clothing. Little did I realize that my mother had been trained as a tailor and made much nicer clothes than they sold in the stores. I was the only girl in the family and she loved making pretty dresses for me. Those beautiful dresses made me feel special and loved by my mother—especially those twirly dresses, the kind that flared out when you spun around.

In Genesis 37:3, we find a father who had something very special sewn for his son. It may not have been twirly, but it was a beautiful coat, either with many colors or with long and flowing sleeves, a piece of clothing that signified royalty. His father had it made for him because he was the son of his most-beloved wife. It signified a position of authority, and this created tension among the brothers. Eventually their jealousy rose to such a boiling point that they planned to kill him. Green with envy, they couldn't see their brother for who he really was, and eventually his own brothers sold him into slavery. They took his beautiful robe, the symbol of his royal status, and dipped it in blood—hoping to make it look as if an animal had killed him. They desecrated the beautiful robe, making it unclean, and declared their brother dead. It would take decades and many life lessons before the family could again be reunited.

I have the privilege of serving the Church of the Nazarene as a general superintendent. Learning the job has been a challenge as I've been changed and stretched in ways I could not have imagined. Each of the six general superintendents has an area of "jurisdiction"— internationally and in the US. My first international assignment was in Africa. This was a real blessing, because my dear brothers and sisters have taught me much about the church and life. This includes many conversations in which we have talked about Jesus and the ways we view him. We all have a particular lens through which we view life, other people, and even our friends.

Dany introduced me to the Nigerian author and novelist Chimamanda Adichie. She speaks in a TED about the danger of what she calls "a single story." She says, "Show people as one thing over and over again, and that's what they become."[16] She warns that we risk critical and cultural misunderstanding when we fail to understand that every life, every situation, has its own overlapping story. What is the danger of a single story? Adichie says,

> The single story creates stereotypes, and the problem with stereotypes is not that they are untrue, but that they are incomplete. When we hear the same story over and over again, it becomes the only story we ever believe. And this stands especially true for the story of Africa. Too often do we hear this version—Africa, the poorest "country" in the world, where only rural landscapes exist and where people live in terror amongst wild animals. Too often do we treat Africa as one narrative, one we have fostered over generations and generations, becoming so institutionalized that even those who graduated from universities will sometimes slip and refer to Africa as a country or their language as "African." This is the danger of a single story, and it brings to mind a quote by American writer Alvin Toffler: "The illiterate of the twenty-first century will not be those who cannot read and write, but those who cannot learn, unlearn, and relearn."[17]

We must learn to unlearn perpetuated stereotypes in order to allow ourselves to see that there is more than this one narrative—to anything, really. Adiche goes on to say, "Stories matter. Many stories matter. Stories have been used to dispossess and to malign, but stories can also be used to empower and to humanize. Stories can break the dignity of a people, but stories can also repair that broken dignity."[18]

16. Chimamanda Adichie, *The Danger of a Single Story,* TED Talk 2009, https://www.ted.com/talks/chimamanda_ngozi_adichie_the_danger_of_a_single_story?language=en.
17. Alvin Toffler, *Future Shock* (New York: Bantam Books, 1970).
18. Adichie, *Danger,* TED Talk.

When we gather as God's people, whether in Africa, South America, Europe, or India, we have a story! But at the same time, we must recognize that this story may not be the same story that some of the church—much of it shaped and marked by Western European and American cultural influences and experiences—embraces. There have been aspects of Euro-American faith that have influenced the ways we have imagined Christ in our own church, and this may be the danger of the single story.

Growing up in Europe, I always saw Jesus as white. I remember moving to Russia and seeing a particular icon of Christ, Image Not-Made-By-Hands, in the Kremlin for the first time. This is one of the earlier icons of the church and the story goes that a particular monk wanted to paint an icon of Christ but was struggling with how to do that. He fasted and prayed, and one night, Christ visited him in his room. Grabbing a towel, Jesus placed the towel over his face, and when he laid it down, there was his face—that of a very dark man.[19] In that moment, I realized that this was probably a much closer representation of the real Christ than what I had created in my imagination.

Without our realizing what's happening, the danger of a single story means that we may begin to form Christ in our own image. This is why we must ask ourselves difficult questions about whether there has been a more dominant story. Frantz Fanon, a writer in postcolonial studies, tells that an inferiority complex develops when there is an "unconscious and unnatural training of black people, from early childhood, to associate 'blackness' with 'wrongness.'"[20] This was illustrated to me when my South African colleagues told me that during

19. "Icon Acheiropoieta," https://en.wikipedia.org/wiki/Acheiropoieta.
20. Fanon, *Black Skin, White Masks.*

Apartheid, young black and colored children wanted to grow up to be white. The danger of a single story begins to unfold when we use a series of colors to tell the gospel story, where black is bad and represents sin, and white is a cleansed heart, and represents all that is good. When we present Christ in a particular way, framed by one culture, we come dangerously close to the possibility of creating an inferiority complex in those who are not from the dominant "Christ culture." From history we find the extreme where many colonialists did not believe that people of color were created in the image of God, and this gave license to treat people of color as if they were not human, using pejoratives such as the "heathen."

Spending time throughout the African continent, I have seen Christ reflected in the beauty of rich diversity. Diversity of worship, song, clothing, language, and culture floods the senses in a church that will soon become the center of gravity for Christianity in this world. Philip Jenkins says Christianity is "a religion that began in ancient Africa and in our lifetime has chosen to go home."[21] Jenkins declares that every denomination in the world is in a state of transition, and the major influence for change will come from the global south to the global north. This is the time to listen to each others' voices and allow God to shape and form us in new ways.

Let me return to Africa where, just like Joseph, I was told the stories of the beauty that was stripped away when millions were sold into slavery and forced to adopt European ways. I stood in the "doorway of no return" on Goree Island in Senegal, the westernmost point of the continent of Africa, where millions were sent off, separated from their loved ones, and treated inhumanely—often by those who called themselves Christians.

21. Philip Jenkins, "The Future of Seminaries and Churches" (San Antonio, Texas, February 9, 2015), to ATS presidents.

In the biblical text, we discover that Joseph's family was struggling to survive. Famine had struck and little by little they were running out of resources. They were starving to death and had to travel to a new land to find food. "They said to one another, 'Alas, we are paying the penalty for what we did to our brother; we saw his anguish when he pleaded with us, but we would not listen. That is why this anguish has come upon us.' Then Reuben answered them, 'Did I not tell you not to wrong the boy? But you would not listen. So now there comes a reckoning for his blood'" (Genesis 42:21–22, NRSV).

What we see is those with the single story are struggling for survival. The white church in America is in decline for every single denomination. The attractional model of church growth encouraged the church to be singular in focus because a homogenous group was supposed to grow faster. At times we compromised and became aligned with powers that we thought might protect the church and help her to feel safe. All of this has been at the expense of our sisters and brothers who have felt alienated and marginalized. What does this mean for a holiness church in this time and place? It means that we must follow the humility of Christ by reaching out to our brothers and sisters who have been at the margins and together make our way back home.

Let's fast forward to the New Testament. In Paul's letter to the church at Ephesus, we find our ecclesiology. This is a glimpse of the kind of church that we are supposed to be. Paul, who was called to be a missionary to the gentiles, often found himself standing up for those who were not quite like him. He realized that he was a man who had been given many advantages in life, and, from a worldly perspective, had numerous reasons to boast. "If anyone else has reason to be confident in the flesh, I have more: circumcised on the eighth day, a member of the people of Israel, of the tribe of Benjamin, a Hebrew born of Hebrews; as to the law, a Pharisee; as to zeal, a persecutor of the church; as to righteousness under the law, blameless. Yet whatever gains I had, these I have come to regard as loss because of Christ" (Philippians 3:4–7, NRSV).

For Paul, Christ became the center point around which the gospel must be focused. Nothing else is of concern for him, except knowing Christ. There are times, however, when we feel that we have been on the margins, and we don't always feel comfortable trying to speak to the powers in the center. On the other hand, there are also those who have been in the center, who, like Paul, have realized that worldly success and power is nothing when compared to Christ. And in Christ the church is to be something new, something different.

Every church has a past, and we are all called to humble ourselves and ask for forgiveness for the times we have not listened, given voice to those who had none, or practiced equality. The good news is that Paul gives us a little glimpse of the hope to be found in the church.

In his letter to the Ephesians Paul wrote:

Although I am the very least of all the saints, this grace was given to me to bring to the Gentiles the news of the boundless riches of Christ, and to make everyone see what is the plan of the mystery hidden for ages in God who created all things; so that through the church the wisdom of God in its rich variety might now be made known to the rulers and authorities in the heavenly places. This was in accordance with the eternal purpose that he has carried out in Christ Jesus our Lord, in whom we have access to God in boldness and confidence through faith in him.

(Ephesians 3:8–12, NRSV)

It becomes clear that the church has a unique role to play in revealing God's mystery. This is a mystery of ministry among all people, which is to usher in a new era. In that moment, the church is transformed, and her actions are suddenly on display for all the world to see. Not only in this world, but spectators in the heavenly realms are focused and intent upon what God is doing through his bride, the church.

What happens in the church is highlighted, as if on center stage, as God's wisdom is manifest in the variegated, multifaceted diversity for all of earth and heaven to see. A lot of other translations miss what's really being said here. They focus on God's wisdom, but the original word for "rich variety" is the same word used in the Greek version of the Old Testament to describe Joseph's coat of many colors. It is only used once in the New Testament, and in this place, it becomes a nuance that allows us to realize that the church has a unique role to play. In the church all things are to be united into one through love. This is a holy unity that witnesses to the love found in the triune God.

The church is part of God's divine plan—no afterthought, but woven into the texture of history from the very beginning. And now, all of God's people are invited, not just as spectators, but also as participants, each playing a role in reflecting the character of God to the world. The church carries on her shoulders a divine responsibility. This is not just some business organization, but the instrument through which Christ has chosen to reveal the mysteries of God to this world. The church is not supposed to be like the world. Instead, she is to be a beautiful patchwork coat with long sleeves, symbols of royalty, made up of the multifaceted diversity of this world that God knits together into the kingdom of God.

What does this look like in the practical sense? We are to be a people, brought together from every nation, tribe, color, and gender and united together in Christ. The church should be able to accomplish what government authorities cannot do. Negotiations for peace, and a mutuality that leads to worship of God, should be highlights of life in the church.

The beautiful coat has been made clean by the blood of the Lamb. We hold in our hands the ability to redeem what has been wounded. It's far too easy to retreat to our comfort zones because change requires work. In reality, many people are in desperate need of Christ and the divine mystery of the church that would transform their lives.

There are lessons to be learned from Joseph's experience. While the white church, and almost any homogenous church, is in decline, there is a divine mystery to be revealed. The divine mystery of the church is in embracing multicultural diversity—black and white, Hispanic and Asian, immigrant and long-standing citizen. This is what the coat of many colors looks like. This is the time for the church to humble herself and realize that she robbed herself of the beautiful diversity that God intended.

What does this future look like? Maybe it looks a little like Marcus Samuelsson. You'll find him on the Food Network. He's an Ethiopian-born, Swedish chef who lives and works in New York City. He's become a famous chef because of his unique ability to bring together the intersections of his life into his food. Adopted by Swedish parents, he traveled the world with his father, who worked as a geologist. Later he spent a year cooking on a cruise ship, learning the flavors of many nations. Coming to New York City, he did something no one else had ever done—he used the foundation of Swedish cooking and added to it the complex tastes he had experienced across the globe—inventing a new type of cuisine that has won him numerous accolades.

This is a season for change, and it must be more than a program—it must become a way of life. Recently, while I was on an airplane, a film was shown about a homeless man in the south and a wealthy businessman who had been drawn into a ministry for the homeless by his wife. As they sat together over a meal at a shelter, the homeless man asked the businessman a few questions.

"What are we doing here? Why are we eating together and where is this going?" He continued, "I hear that people like you enjoy going fishing, only you do it for sport. You catch fish, look them over, and then put them back in the water."

The businessman replied, "Yes, we call it catch and release."

The homeless man went on, "Let me tell you what we used to do where I grew up. When we went fishing it was with purpose. We wanted to catch the best fish that we could that day, and when we had one, we would reel it in and then carry it home. All the way home we stopped to show our friends what we had caught. Arriving home we proudly showed off the fish to our mother, who gladly prepared it for dinner. We invited our friends to join us and to enjoy what we had caught. So, let me ask you again what we're doing here. Is this 'catch and release,' or are you going to take me home?"

For far too long we have had programs and emphases that taught us to catch and release. Real change means that we must take one another home, practice genuine hospitality, and incorporate our brothers and sisters into our lives, proudly sharing them with our friends and neighbors.

Then Joseph could no longer control himself before all those who stood by him, and he cried out, "Send everyone away from me." So no one stayed with him when Joseph made himself known to his brothers. And he wept so loudly that the Egyptians heard it, and the household of Pharaoh heard it. Joseph said to his brothers, "I am Joseph. Is my father still alive?" But his brothers could not answer him, so dismayed were they at his presence. Then Joseph said to his brothers, "Come closer to me." And they came closer. He said, "I am your brother, Joseph, whom you sold into Egypt."

(Genesis 45:1–4, NRSV)

We all love who we are and where we have come from, but God wants to take what we have been and add to it, making something new and better. This is a new day of multiculturalism that knits us together as a people of God and brings us to a place where we speak to the powers and authorities of this world in new ways. Our prayer is that we can be a people of holy boldness, embracing one another in the love of God. The scenes played out will not be in harmony with those of the world, but are intended to leave the spectators in awe of the church of Jesus Christ!

I want to see the church put on that beautiful coat—the twirly one, with many colors and long sleeves. This won't be easy and the change has to begin with me. My view of Jesus has expanded because I have been blessed to encounter my brothers and sisters from around the world. The likeness of Jesus Christ, the image of God, is reflected in every person that God has created, and the more that we get to know one another the more we get to know Christ. Suddenly my Jesus is not just white, but encompasses every dazzling color found in creation.

The words of Alvin Toffler ring in my ears: "The illiterate of the twenty-first century will not be those who cannot read and write, but those who cannot learn, unlearn, and relearn." This is a call to repentance, a place of weeping and groaning loudly for where we have been, believing that God will embrace us with his holy love, reuniting us and covering us again with his royal robe.

QUESTIONS FOR REFLECTION

1. Close your eyes and imagine Jesus. Describe what he looks like.

_____

_____

_____

2. How would you describe your single story?

_____

_____

_____

3. What experiences have you had with diversity that have helped to broaden your understanding of God?

_____

_____

_____

4. How would you explain God's plan for the church?

_____

_____

_____

5. Close your eyes again, and now, imagine what your church could look like.

_____

_____

_____

6. What does it mean for you personally to learn, unlearn, and relearn?

_____

_____

_____

4

YELLOW

Hospitality

Dany and Carla

The rays of the giant yellow sun filled the afternoon sky. We were bouncing along in a bus, on our way to meet with new believers in a small village in West Africa, in the country of Guinea Bissau. We could feel the dust on our teeth as the dirt-packed road rose to meet us. There in the distance were houses made from bricks that were drying in the heat of the day.

Under the large tree, the people of the village had already gathered, singing and dancing to the drumbeat, ready to show hospitality to their visitors. Children warmly surrounded us as we exited the bus and were invited into the school. There, a full presentation had been prepared; the children sang songs, recited stories, and thanked the church for the education they were receiving. Since we were the special guests, our hosts provided us with gifts, including live chickens. They were large, beautiful chickens, and we hated to take them, but it was important for our hosts to show us hospitality. You see, if we are going to learn from one another, then we must be willing to receive from one another. On one occasion you may be the host, on another, the guest.

The color yellow reminds us of the warmth of hospitality. In Luke 10:38–42, we find the story of Jesus's encounter with Mary and Martha. While it appears that Martha is criticized in this story, there is also much to learn about hospitality. Whether the radiant heat from the sun or the yellow reflection of gold, hospitality reminds us that we are to treat our guests with warmth, just as we would royalty. The reality is that Martha was showing Jesus hospitality by the way he was welcomed into the home. For Martha, hospitality was all about cooking and providing the best food. Her sister, Mary, seemed to have a different idea about hospitality, having to do with attentiveness to the guest's teachings. Both of them probably thought they were doing the right thing, and both were showing hospitality. Jesus was asking Martha whether she was willing to learn that there was more to hospitality than what happens in the kitchen. What Martha failed to realize was that the best dish in the house was being served in the front room where Jesus was teaching. Martha needed to humble herself to learn more about the ways she could show hospitality, and that may have been by taking on the role of the guest, for Jesus, the Master, was in the house.

Martha probably viewed herself as the expert on hospitality. She was ready to teach Jesus what hospitality really meant, and she was sure her sister was wrong. For years, Martha had played the role of hostess and no one, not even Jesus, was going to change her understanding of how to do things. This is how the person from the dominant culture often responds in new situations. Always having served as the host, it becomes uncomfortable to take the role of the guest. However, if we are going to learn from one another, we must be willing to receive from one another. When you have been invited to be the guest, then you must respond and know your place. There is an African saying that serves as a great reminder, "The guest does not untie the goat."

We enjoy inviting friends over for dinner and preparing special meals. Sometimes we work for hours to prepare for a special occasion. Can you imagine that the moment arrives when you invite your guests to the table, only to have them run back out to the car to get something. Before sitting down to eat, they produce their own cutlery and dishes, rearranging everything that has already been set. In that moment, we feel dejected, as if we have done a poor job of hosting.

Sadly, this is how we have often entered new cultures. We come with many things because we believe that what we have brought with us is something that *they* should have. We don't arrive empty-handed as a guest so our hosts can take care of us, but instead, we feel the need to show people something we think is better. There is vulnerability in being the guest, for you are now dependent upon the host.

We are to take on the role of the guest and go and enjoy that which is prepared for us. Early in the Gospel of Mark we read about Jesus being a guest in the home of Simon and Andrew. He doesn't enter the home and take over, but he goes with them and listens to what they have to say. Maybe they were concerned that they could not provide for Jesus in the way that they would have liked because they tell Jesus that Simon's mother-in-law is sick in bed with a fever. Jesus goes to her and takes her by the hand, lifts her from the bed, and the fever disappears immediately. The story ends with, "and she began to serve them" (Mark 1:31, NRSV; see also vv. 29–30). Jesus didn't become the host, but he made it possible for them to fulfill their role as hosts, while he remained the guest.

Jesus had experience being a guest. During the early years of his life, he and his parents lived in Egypt, where his hosts provided protection from Herod. Early on, he learned traditions that were different from those of his parents, and the foods he ate would not have been those his mother would have normally prepared. Even the games he played with other children would not have been the same as those in Nazareth. All of these experiences helped to prepare Jesus for the journey ahead and for modeling a life of humble hospitality.

Later, in the book of Revelation, we find Jesus standing at the door and knocking. He refuses to force himself upon the people, and instead he says, "Listen! I am standing at the door, knocking; if you hear my voice and open the door, I will come in to you and eat with you, and you with me" (Revelation 3:20, NRSV). Jesus awaits the hospitality of the people and refuses to force himself into the home. While he may be the king, he will not use his power or authority to open the door. Instead, he awaits the hospitality of those in the household. The desire for a relationship of mutuality is expressed when he says that he will eat with them, and they will eat with him. Around the table there is a give and take, a learning and sharing from one another, and this becomes the vision of hospitality that we receive from Christ. When we fail to live into this hospitality, then the colors within the beautiful coat become skewed and overwhelmingly monochromatic.

This type of hospitality gives us a different perspective of mission. The attitude of the guest is to be the same as that of Jesus Christ who emptied himself and became like a servant. This is the picture of Jesus that is painted for us by the apostle Paul in Philippians 2, where he writes about the humility of Christ. "Who, though he was in the form of God, did not regard equality with God as something to be exploited" (Philippians 2:6, NRSV). This verse is foundational to the early church's understanding about the nature of Jesus. Paul was expressing a thought that would be significant for the Christian faith. Jesus was not just in the image of God, but Jesus was the very "nature" or "form" of God. He wasn't something "like" God, but he was of the very same "substance" as God. Jesus is the Son of God, and therefore is ruler over all the heavens and the earth. He is the king, and yet his behavior becomes a model of humility and hospitality.

As the story of Jesus's hospitality unfolds, we are continually reminded of Jesus's status. While he has all wealth, authority, and power at his disposal as a member of royalty, he refuses to use anything for his own benefit. He doesn't grasp or cling to what he has been given, but he chooses to give it away, emptying himself of all that is rightfully his. He is willing to share his power with others so that all of humanity might become heirs to the throne. He refuses to continually act as the host but willingly becomes a guest so that others may share in his resources and they may serve as host.

For the church in Philippi this idea was quite shocking. This was a Roman colony, and they were accustomed to Roman rulers who were constantly fighting, cheating, and killing to obtain power. They were known to have killed their own relatives in order to maintain control, power, and wealth. Therefore, Jesus's model of hospitality was entirely foreign, for while he was God and had all rights to his status, he refused to abuse his power, showing no selfish ambition and sharing his power for good. The unselfish nature of Jesus's act of hospitality is a pattern for all of us to follow. There is to be no exploitation of power, position, race, or culture in our lives. We are never to use what we possess in an unfair or selfish way.

Sadly, this is not always the motivation found in our hearts. Our sinful nature drives us to selfishness and a manipulation of situations and circumstances for our own good. Paul has emphasized that Jesus has the same nature as God, and this, then, becomes an invitation for us to be found "in Christ." When we participate in the hospitality of Christ, then we are to be found "in" Christ as partakers of the divine nature. It is only then that by nature, there is no longer a desire to exploit. This is a deep-seated change that is needed in the heart of an individual and among God's gathered people, the church. This divine hospitality is to be the way a holiness church—individually and collectively—engages with the world.

We had spent the entire day traveling to Ethiopia and had gone through airport security at least six times. Our feet were filthy from the dirty floors we had walked on, and when we arrived at the hotel, there was no running water and no way to get cleaned up before the evening service. Having done the best we could, we headed out for a time of worship with our church leaders. We were taken by car to the district center, and when we entered, we were amazed at the sight. The people, most of whom were refugees from South Sudan, had lined the dirt pathway with palm branches. They were singing songs of praise to the Lord and ushered us into the courtyard where chairs, alongside basins of water, were awaiting us. We were asked to be seated, and then they removed our sandals and washed our dirty feet. What a humbling experience to have these sisters and brothers in Christ, who have so little in terms of material goods, provide us with such hospitality. Something inside of us wanted to tell them, "No, no, you don't need to do this," but the smiles on their faces reminded us that we were to humbly accept this act of love, receiving it with a gracious spirit of acceptance.

In Paul's letter to the Ephesians he spoke about hospitality in the form of mutual submission among believers, and specifically in Christian marriage. Just as Jesus knocks on the door, asking for the opportunity to share a meal at the table, so we are to take this mutuality into marriage relationships. In much of the world, culture has had a strong influence on our understanding of marriage. With Jesus as the model for humility and hospitality, we see these scriptures in a whole new light.

Ephesians 5 is a clear admonition for all of God's children to imitate God and live a life of love. All relationships are to be patterned after the hospitality that is found in the triune God, where mutual submission and humility become the ultimate acts of holy love. Within this understanding of hospitality, Paul uses marriage as a practical example for God's people: "Wives, be subject to your husbands as you are to the Lord. . . . Husbands, love your wives, just as Christ loved the church and gave himself up for her" (Ephesians 5:22, 25, NRSV). This is the same pattern we find in the relationship between the Father, the Son, and the Holy Spirit. God's intention is that this hospitality should be witnessed in marriage. At the same time, marriage is to reflect the relationship between Christ and the church, or the bridegroom and the bride. A Christian marriage is to be one that reflects the hospitality of God to the world, and in many cases, this may be countercultural. In much of the world there continue to be struggles within marriage and family relationships where there is no mutuality.

Family relations can be extremely complex, and these become compounded when different cultures are brought into the marriage relationship. Often culture becomes the loudest voice when it comes to influencing the ways men and women treat one another. Add to this the complexity of intermarriage among different religions, and a marriage marked by Christian hospitality faces great opposition. At the same time, Christian marriage can be a microcosm of God's intention for beautiful diversity within the church.

The mutuality of women and men within the kingdom is a sign of God's intent for restoration. This is why the image of women being mutually engaged in marriage and in the work of the kingdom is vital. The prophet Isaiah could see a future in which God's people would be completely restored: "No longer will they call you Deserted, or name your land Desolate. But you will be called Hephzibah, and your land Beulah; for the LORD will take delight in you, and your land will be married" (Isaiah 62:4). The "land" referred to the people of God in exile, but for us it becomes a metaphor for the church. The church will not be deserted, nor will it be filled with ruins. Instead, the land, or the church, will again be filled with God's people—the people being called "Hephzibah," or "I delight in you." This was the name of King Hezekiah's wife, and the two of them, Hezekiah and Hephzibah, represented a period of faithfulness in loving service to the Lord. The call is for the people of God to reflect a marriage in which there is mutual hospitality. The land itself, or the church, will be restored and will be known as "Beulah"—which means married, because it is entirely consecrated to God in all of her beauty and diversity—married to him, and God finds this delightful.

The imagery of marriage is found throughout Scripture, from beginning to end. In Genesis, we are drawn into the marriage scene between the first couple, Adam and Eve. In the intervening books, we continually see God loving his people and drawing them into a covenant relationship with him. Sadly, humanity continues to commit adultery and the relationships crumble. That's why the imagery of Christian marriage is vital in the world, because it provides a visual model of the hope of humanity. The beauty of marriage is found at the end of the journey, in Revelation:

> Then I heard what seemed to be the voice of a great multitude, like the sound of many waters and like the sound of mighty thunderpeals, crying out, "Hallelujah! For the Lord our God the Almighty reigns. Let us rejoice and exult and give him the glory, for the marriage of the Lamb has come, and his bride has made herself ready; to her it has been granted to be clothed with fine linen, bright and pure"—for the fine linen is the righteous deeds of the saints. And the angel said to me, "Write this: Blessed are those who are invited to the marriage supper of the Lamb." And he said to me, "These are true words of God."
>
> (Revelation 19:6–9, NRSV)

Cultural attacks on God's intent for marriage may signify something happening at an even deeper level. Could it be that the self-centeredness of humanity doesn't allow us to be in or to make a serious commitment to marriage? When this happens, we see moral decay across the spectrum. There is no hospitality of Christ to be revealed to the world, when there is no hospitality in marriage.

Cultural influences go beyond marriage, and affect the ways we think about women. We were in West Africa, talking to a district superintendent about his life. He was very sad that day because it was the one-year anniversary of his wife's death. He had been left alone, a widower, with five children. He expressed gratitude for his sister, who had recently come to live with him and help take care of his home and children. While he served as district superintendent, he also pastored a local church. We asked him questions about his ministry and were amazed when he told us that he thought he had around four hundred churches on his district but wasn't sure of the exact number because new ones were being planted every day. This one district has more than thirty thousand members—the largest district anywhere in the Church of the Nazarene. Curious, we wanted to know how this happened, and he began to tell us about how the women were his evangelists and church planters. Every day as they went to the market or to get water, they told everyone they met about Jesus. They had scarves printed with pictures of the gospel story so they could wear them and then lay them on the ground to tell people about Jesus.

The rapid expansion of the church in Benin is primarily because women refuse to live in fear of their culture, and they tell everyone they meet about Jesus. Not only are they evangelists, but they also routinely plant churches in their homes. These women have intentionally chosen to participate in the work of the kingdom of God. They have learned mutual hospitality and live in the power and strength of the Holy Spirit.

Women's service and ordination in the church comes from our doctrine of holiness and is one of the golden threads that holds together the beautiful colors of the church. This is not culturally dictated but is foundational to who we are as a people of God. When the work of the Church of the Nazarene began in the Democratic Republic of the Congo (DRC) our leaders were told that women would never be allowed to be ordained. Our regional director responded that the culture would not dictate what happens in the life of the church and that, without women's ordination, there would be no church in the DRC. In January of 2017, we were able to be present in Goma in the Northern Kivu area of the DRC and ordain twenty-one individuals, three of whom were women. The entire congregation celebrated this groundbreaking moment in the life of the church and the way this act reflected the hospitality of Christ.

In Senegal, there is a tradition that when the evening meal is prepared, there is always enough for an extra plate. This plate remains in the kitchen in a covered dish, and it is called the "fool's meal." It is left there in case a guest might come during the night and need something to eat. There should always be something available, because the spirit of hospitality means that a meal is always prepared to welcome a guest. We, as God's people, should always be ready for the guest, the one who is coming from far away—whether physically or culturally—prepared to make them feel welcome and to share what we have with them.

The writer to the Hebrews wrote about this hospitality, and again, it is couched in the language of mutuality and love: "Let mutual love continue. Do not neglect to show hospitality to strangers, for by doing that some have entertained angels without knowing it" (Hebrews 13:1–2, NRSV). The warmth of hospitality and the glow of holy love do a work that is beyond what we may imagine. In the movie *The Mission,* the priest comes to a village with absolutely nothing. He sits down and begins to play his flute and through this song, played in humility for he has nothing else to offer, the missionary becomes the guest that God is able to use.

God wants us to depend upon him, and he chose to come to earth as a baby. The incarnation is itself hospitality, for God came into our human culture in a human body. Now, God is depending on us. We are to humbly enter another culture in bodily form, emptying ourselves and embracing what we encounter, by sitting at the table in a spirit of hospitality.

QUESTIONS FOR REFLECTION

1. How do you practice hospitality in your culture?

_____

_____

2. What programs have we had that have led us to "catch and release"?

_____

_____

3. How would you interpret, "The guest does not untie the goat"? Give examples of times when you may have unintentionally done this.

_____

_____

4. Are we comfortable taking on the role of the guest, and if not, what are our own obstacles?

_____

_____

5. How is unleashing women for ministry a hospitable act?

_____

_____

5

PURPLE

Identity

Dany and Carla

When crossing an international border, you have to carry your passport. This is the document that proves your identity, telling the world who you are and where you have come from. These are labels that have been given to us by the world. Dany carries two passports, one Senegalese and the other French. He easily moves from one language to the next and even one identity to the other, depending on the context. Carla has a German birth certificate but is a dual United States and Canadian citizen. She has a distinctly American accent when speaking English but becomes a bit of a chameleon when slipping into Russian or German. All of these are markers that the world uses to peg one's identity and somehow push each individual into a particular mold so that the boxes can be ticked on immigration forms.

In reality, identity isn't all that easy for us to clarify. Each one of us has the potential of a myriad of identities, depending upon the context or situation. Dany carries the additional identities of a minister, a teacher, a musician, a regional director, a brother, a husband, and a father. Carla is also a minister, a teacher, a nurse, a general superintendent, a sister, a wife, a mother, and a grandmother. There are many forces that shape and forge our identities and that can create confusion, while at the same time, there are places where we find commonality.

Let's take a moment to look at race, which is one of the boxes we have to tick on those immigration forms. The world would tell us that this is a major cause of difference between individuals and that the color of our skin is what creates our identity. In reality, the human race shares a genome that is 99.5% identical, with the amount of melanin accounting for a fraction of the difference in humans.[22] There is only one race, the human race, and we are almost all genetically alike. The world has created divisions in humanity because of a chemical in our bodies that makes one person's skin darker than another. Is this really what makes up our identity, or is there something else that is at work in our lives?

That dreaded moment had arrived—we were to go in and view my brother's body. I, Carla, stood with my father, holding his hand as we slowly entered the small chapel. He walked gingerly, taking small steps toward the viewing area. Along the way my father looked at me and said, "This is hard. No parent should ever have to bury their child."

I looked into his eyes and saw the lines of grief on his face. Together we peered into the casket of my oldest brother, the one who bore my father's name. There was nothing about

22. Susan Mayor, "Genome Sequence of One Individual Is Published for the First Time." *BMJ*, September 15, 2007.

this moment that was as it should have been, but the depth of love that came from my father's heart is something that I will never forget.

Most people hardly realized that my oldest brother was not the biological son of my parents. He was adopted when he was only a few days old and spent his entire life as a member of the household. My parents would not have imagined that he was anything other than a full member of the family. Somehow his arrival changed things, and three biological children eventually filled the home. The four children, all bearing the family name, but the oldest with our father's name, were equally loved and shepherded by our parents. From the day he arrived until the day he was buried, my brother lived in the overflow of love that he received from his mother and father. He had been fully adopted into the family.

Just imagine children from all over the globe; people of every race and ethnicity, gathered together into the Father's house. Our heavenly Father has provided a way for the adoption of us all into his family. The love of an earthly father is nothing in comparison to what our Father in heaven wants to lavish on us.

Just like the women of Benin, Jesus was a master storyteller. The parables we find in the New Testament are vivid pictures that speak to the cultures of the world, drawing us into his story. We see a Father standing on the side of the road, looking off longingly into the distance, hoping and praying that his long-lost son will come home. His son has traded his identity for a chance at survival, and when he realizes he has nothing left, he comes back home. In humility he is willing to accept the identity of a servant, just so that he will have something to eat. The father, however, is not concerned that his son has thrown away all that he had, for the father has the power to restore everything—including his identity. The father catches a glimpse of his son off in the distance, for he recognizes the gait and the way he carries his shoulders. This is his boy! Unable to contain his joy, he runs toward his son, throws his arms around him in a warm embrace, and welcomes him back home and into the family.

As a sign of that welcome, the father calls for the best robe to be given to his son, symbolizing that the power and authority of his birthright, and identity, has been restored. The beautiful promise in this parable reaches out beyond the story of a lost, Middle Eastern, Jewish boy. Jesus wanted all who heard the story to know that his Father was also their Father. Whether black or white, Senegalese or American, the promise reaches out beyond this son and to all those who will intersect with the parable. Our heavenly Father stands out on the road day after day, facing in our direction, ready to wrap us in his royal robes of purple, restoring to us all the privileges of the family.

But why robes of purple? There is something extremely fascinating about the color purple, for it has a long history. The most famous is called Tyrian purple and was discovered by the Phoenicians about 1,500 years before the birth of Christ. The dye is produced by sea snails called the murex, found in the Mediterranean Sea. The beauty of the color is notable, along with the fact that it does not fade but intensifies over time with exposure to the sun.

Historically purple fabric could only be afforded by the wealthiest of society, for it took nearly 12,000 snails to produce an ounce of color. For more than 3,000 years, the color purple has been associated with royalty. When we become active participants in the kingdom of God, we are wrapped in the Father's royal robes, invited into an experience of God's expansive beauty.

Sadly, throughout the centuries, the church has co-opted the color purple for its own benefit. Wanting to adopt the power structures of the world, the bishops of the church began dressing themselves in purple. This is a subtle reminder that the potential for corruption exists, even among those who may consider themselves a part of God's family. Our identity as a member of God's family must always be evident by our behaviors, which mimic the life of Christ. The family resemblance does not come from the color of our skin, the clothes we wear, or the language we speak, but from the ways we interact with one another, reflecting the nature and love found in God.

This life in Christ takes us on a journey away from subdued tones into one where we see glorious imagery stretched before us, with vivid flashes of color and the joyful sound of music. This is where we are all invited to live as a royal priesthood. Every person lives with the potential of being robed in the beauty of the Father's royal garments. As God's people, we all discover a new identity; we are each a child of the Father, we are chosen, "a royal priesthood, a holy nation, God's special possession, . . . declar[ing] the praises of him who called [us] out of darkness into his wonderful light" (1 Peter 2:9).

The boxes on the immigration forms do not define us. God's children are identified by the robe of royalty, which is intended to envelop every aspect of life. The world's barriers are dissolved as God's beloved children are revealed to the world. "See what love the Father has given us, that we should be called children of God; and that is what we are. The reason the world does not know us is that it did not know him. Beloved, we are God's children now; what we will be has not yet been revealed. What we do know is this: when he is revealed, we will be like him, for we will see him as he is. And all who have this hope in him purify themselves, just as he is pure" (1 John 3:1–3, NRSV).

A poor little Jewish girl, living in the Middle East, gave birth to a baby in a stable, and she had to lay the baby in a manger for his cradle. The birth of the little child, Jesus, makes the adoption of all others possible. Jesus lived his entire life in such a way that he could provide a pathway back to the Father for all the rest of us to follow. This pathway to the Father leads to restoration and transformation. Adopted children are transformed by the holy love of the Father and begin to take on a family resemblance.

God's Son is our brother. The one who was born in a humble setting among the animals is the one we are to follow. New life is breathed into our lungs and we find a new identity, which is to be lived out in the kingdom of God. Little by little, brothers and sisters from every nation begin to reflect the holiness of Jesus as they have been gathered into the Father's robes.

For centuries, missionaries have carried the good news of the gospel around the world, inviting people from many nations to become a part of the family. Today the family has expanded beyond our imagination as people from every nation and tongue are responding to the call to become a part of the royal priesthood. Clothed in purple, we find God's people on the move, declaring the praises of the one who has called us out of darkness.

Frankfurt, Germany, has become a crossroads of international migration. The result is a new multicultural diversity that has never been seen before. The church is working in an ever-changing environment and will never look quite the same as it did in the past. Coming together around the Lord's Table are people from many different lands—Syria, Iran, Poland, Nigeria—all united as family members in the kingdom of God.

There, a local pastor has discovered a way to respond to the question of identity. When asked, "Are you German?" the new citizens say no. But if they are asked, "Are you a Frankfurter?" they say yes. There is something in the new identity of being a Frankfurter that is acceptable since it is synonymous with this new multicultural world.

If these new citizens are embracing their identity as Frankfurters, maybe this should say something about those who have a new citizenship in the kingdom of God. We are to participate in the work of the new kingdom and her citizens, being united from far and wide through the grace and mercy of Jesus Christ. Having become like Christ, we begin to live in countercultural ways. No longer are we partisans, for we are far too busy being engaged in kingdom activity. Whether the child of God is in Frankfurt or in Goma, DRC, a new identity is defined by our relationship to Christ. The more time we spend with Christ, the more that we become like Christ, and we live into our new identity.

A sense of identity is vital for every one of us. Maslow suggested that when the basic human needs were met, questions of belonging and identity could be addressed.[23] At Maslow's higher levels of belonging, esteem, and self-actualization, we grapple with a myriad of questions related to identity. An expanded version of Maslow's Hierarchy would suggest that after self-actualization comes transcendence, which includes participation in mystery, which includes the spiritual life. We don't reach this level if we are distracted by and attached to the world. When the things of this world become our focus, then the world becomes the center by which we define ourselves. The problem is that by "defining ourselves by virtue of things

23. Saul McLeod, "Maslow's Hierarchy of Need," *Simple Psychology,* https://www.simplypsychology.org/maslow.html.

impermanent, we become lost to ourselves and lose our point of reference for our being in the world."[24] Only by transcending the things of this world and remaining conscious that our core identity comes from the Father we can become all that we were created to be.

Even within the life of the church, we find impermanent identities. These may be the positions that we fill or labels that are put upon us by others. Carla answered her call to preach when she was nearly forty years old. Suddenly, she was labeled by a new identity. This was not just the identity of a preacher, but of a "woman clergy." Little did she know that this identity contained certain boundaries within the life of the church. This was especially true when the identity was combined with that of wife and mother. There was a perception that these identities were somehow in conflict with one another: Surely, one identity needed to be subservient to the other. This was more of a cultural construct than it was a reality related to identity.

The church must be careful not to adopt the standards of this world. Unfortunately, this can happen far too easily, and the transcendence of the kingdom can become elusive. On one occasion Carla was to ordain a young woman as an elder. When she arrived at the assembly, the report was read that she was to be ordained as a deacon. The woman herself was stunned and had no idea what had happened. Questions were raised from the assembly floor as to why the recommendation of elder had been changed to deacon. It was discovered that the woman was single, and Carla was told that in this culture, a single woman could not be an ordained elder. The response was from culture and not from the kingdom.

24. Michael J. Formica, "Examining Our Sense of Identity and Who We Are" in *Psychology Today*, https://www.psychologytoday.com/us/blog/enlightened-living/200910/examining-our-sense-identity-and-who-we-are.

Unfortunately, when the church takes her cues from society, her members will not be able to live out their full identities as children of God. The good news in this situation is that members of the assembly spoke up for what they saw as unjust. They voted to correct the report, and later that day the woman was ordained an elder.

Identity markers that are not provided by our heavenly Father have been used to create division in the world and in the church. The history of apartheid in the Church of the Nazarene is one such example, where the church in South Africa was divided into black, white, and colored. The church must examine herself and work to always and consistently identify all of God's children as true royalty, with equal authority given by the Father. Within the kingdom of God there should be no dominant culture, which has been so easily defined by the world.

Upon reflection, we recognize that at times we have allowed culture to define our understanding of the kingdom of God. The result is the subtle development of a dominant culture. Most fail to see that they have become a part of this culture, for it simply seeps into society and becomes the norm. This can happen anywhere in the world where there is a strong cultural norm, and we fail to recognize that it may be overriding God's kingdom culture. The lens through which we see the world is easily shaped by social mores, and in our naiveté, we may not recognize that we have become judgmental. When we find ourselves asking, "Why don't they do things like we do?" then we are judging from the perspective of a dominant culture. The witness of the church is damaged when emphasis is placed upon adaptation to culture, and not on life in the kingdom of God.

Years ago, Moravian missionaries came to the Ohio region of the Americas to minister to the indigenous people. While they presented Christ, they also brought with them a cultural expectation of life in the kingdom of God. The Native Americans who came to know Christ were expected to wear Western clothing, speak German, live in brick or log houses, and adopt "Christian" names.

There is great danger in this perspective. Speaking on apartheid in South Africa, Steve Biko said, "A man who succeeds in making a group of people accept a foreign concept in which he is expert makes them perpetual students whose progress in the particular field can only be evaluated by him; the student must constantly turn to him for guidance and promotion."[25]

In this way the dominant culture actually exerts power and control, setting all the rules, standards, and templates for success. In a subtle way, "The majority voice does not have to explain itself to outsiders. It's the work of the minority to do all the translation and the accommodation."[26]

When we fail to see that we may be part of a dominant culture, a problem arises. There is not just a single dominant culture in the world but many dominant cultures, depending on one's geographic location. Cultural understandings have infused many of our beliefs, and this includes our theological understandings. In an 1899 edition of *Punch* magazine, we find a joke regarding the U.S. Patent Office: "A genius asked, 'Isn't there a clerk who can examine patents?' A boy replied, 'Quite unnecessary, sir. Everything that can be invented has been invented.'"[27] The magazine was poking fun at the notion

25. Steve Biko, *I Write What I Like: A Selection of His Writings* (Johannesburg: Heinemann Publishers, 1978), 94.

26. "Christendom Is Crumbling and It's Not Pretty: A True Story of Christian Persecution of Christians," *Missio Alliance*, June 2018, https://www.missioalliance.org/christendom-crumbling-not-pretty-true-story-christian-persecution-christians/.

27. Dennis Crouch, "Tracing the Quote: Everything That Can Be Invented Has Been Invented," *Patent Blog*, https://patentlyo.com/patent/2011/01/tracing-the-quote-everything-that-can-be-invented-has-been-invented.html.

that, heading into the twentieth century, people thought so highly of all that had been accomplished that they couldn't imagine there was more to come. Sometimes we may think that the church has done so well that we fail to think there may be more to come.

Since Jesus's commissioning of his disciples, believers have served as agents of the gospel. The apostle Paul crossed from Asia into Europe, shouldering the burden of cross-cultural ministry in the early years of Christianity. In the last centuries, missionaries have carried the message of salvation from one culture to another, commonly speaking of the debt that was paid by Jesus upon the cross. When identity comes from a culture in which money or currency is valued, then the idea of a debt being paid is significant. In a society that does not connect money with spiritual questions, this concept may be entirely foreign. At the same time, the vision of a victorious Christ on the cross conquering evil is easily embraced. Every missionary has to wrestle with the way in which they present the gospel. Paul's sermon on Mars Hill seems to illustrate his adaptability and recognition that he could not preach a Jewish sermon to a group of Greeks in the city of Athens.

Our understanding of identity has also affected the way the message of holiness has been shared to the world. The vision of the founder of the Church of the Nazarene, Dr. Phineas F. Bresee, was that the church would "spread scriptural holiness" around the globe.[28] Much missionary expansion occurred after the Second World War, at a time when the sending church was struggling with holiness and legalism. The holiness message was exported and, at times, became frozen in

---

28. Ernest Alexander Girvin, *Phineas F. Bresee: A Prince in Israel, a Biography* (Kansas City: Pentecostal Nazarene Publishing House, 1916), 218.

a kind of time capsule brought by the missionary who first encountered the new culture.

Interestingly, today one might encounter a local church in South Africa that feels like an American church of the 1960s. The local people were rarely afforded the privilege of reading the original sources and understanding the writings of Wesley, and thereby interpreting holiness within their context.

It was easy for holiness to be understood as transactional or legalistic. The lists of don'ts soon followed, and a church with a powerful message became hidden in fear, increasingly closed-off from the world. Instead of allowing holiness to flourish within the context, too much depended on the teaching of the dominant culture. The current state of affairs could leave us in a state of quandary, wondering how we are to reach a world that desperately needs to know about the power found in the holiness of Jesus Christ while we are recovering from our fears. The answer is found in rediscovery of identity as God's holy people, wrapped in the Father's robes and living in the power of the kingdom.

The ordination service in the Church of the Nazarene is one of our sacred moments where we celebrate the life of the church. As a part of our tradition we normally sing an old American hymn, "Called unto Holiness." This song is difficult to translate into other languages and cultures, and the rhythm is quite a challenge. Often a translator will listen to the original version and then try to rewrite it and place it into their culture. As a result, the song can be heard in a variety of ways, but influenced by the dominant culture.

Recently there was an ordination service in a new world area of the Church of the Nazarene, where no one had ever heard the song. The musicians received the lyrics but had no idea what the song was supposed to sound like, so they just made it up. As the band began to play, the song took on the local culture with the sounds and rhythms of the people. The song was embraced as their own as they learned to sing the words from their hearts, because it was now theirs. As Christianity engages with culture, we will see real beauty and depth of understanding unfold, for this is God's plan. True identity reflects beauty when set free within the kingdom of God.

When our identity is "in" Christ, then we are also to "put on" Christ. The apostle Paul admonished the church in Philippi to have the same mind as Jesus: "Let the same mind be in you that was in Christ Jesus, who, though he was in the form of God, did not regard equality with God as something to be exploited, but emptied himself, taking the form of a slave, being born in human likeness. And being found in human form, he humbled himself and became obedient to the point of death—even death on a cross" (Philippians 2:5–8, NRSV).

This section of Scripture is referred to as the *kenosis* (self-emptying) passage, where Jesus does not seek to retain his position, but willingly empties himself for the sake of the kingdom. He doesn't exploit what he has, but he intentionally shares his power with others, so that we, too, can become heirs to the throne. Paul reiterated this point because, by nature, we have a hard time with this concept. Our nature is to be selfish and to want to use others for our own benefit. This is why he emphasized that Jesus has the same nature as God—and that we are invited to be "in" Christ or to participate in the divine nature. When this happens, then, by nature, there is no longer a desire to exploit. This is a deep-seated change in the heart of an individual brought about by the presence of Christ.

This brings us back to the significance of the incarnation. It is only because Jesus was God but chose to become human, that we as humans can participate in the nature of God. If this is possible, then cultural Christianity falls miserably short of providing satisfaction in life. Why settle for cultural Christianity when we follow a Messiah who came to earth so that we can become like him? Jesus willingly shares his inheritance with those who are adopted into the family because he refuses to exploit what he has for his own good.

We are called to have this same attitude and to adopt the humble posture of *kenosis*, where we intentionally submit any identity that is temporal and derived from the world to that which is found as God's child. This is just as difficult for those who are part of the dominant culture as it is for those who are not.

The transcendent identity we receive from being found in Christ will always be under attack because it is foundational to our being. All of God's children are invited to live in glorious freedom, released from identities placed upon us by the world. In our adoption, we embrace the words of John, "So if the Son makes you free, you will be free indeed" (John 8:36, NRSV).

The enemy chose to attack Christ by questioning his identity. In the Gospel of Matthew, we read: "The tempter came and said to him, 'If you are the Son of God, command these stones to become loaves of bread.' But he answered, 'It is written, "One does not live by bread alone, but by every word that comes from the mouth of God"'" (Matthew 4:3–4, NRSV). In attacking Jesus's identity, the enemy knew that Jesus would lose his freedom. Jesus was and is the Son of God. Matthew mirrored the temptation scene with that of Jesus on the cross. The bystanders shouted at him, "You who would destroy the temple and build it in three days, save yourself! *If you are the Son of God*, come down from the cross" (Matthew 27:40, NRSV, emphasis added). Again—his identity was questioned, but Jesus was never deterred. He rejected any identity that the world may have given him and clung to the Father. In his Sonship, we find our adoption, wrapped in the robes of royalty, free to be who we were meant to be in Christ.

Our mindset is changed and we no longer live as slaves, but in freedom and power as one who is the child of a king.

The question of identity brings us to an understanding of truth. Jesus's identity was found in the truth that he was the Son of God. So vital was this to the faith of the disciples that Jesus would stop from time to time and ask them, "Who do you say that I am?" This truth was bound in the age-old scriptures that had been foundational to the covenant between Israel and their identity as God's people. Jesus found himself in the wilderness just as the Israelites had so many years before. That is where the Israelites struggled with their identity as God's people, tempted by all that Egypt and the rest of the world had to offer them. In contrast to Moses, they refused to trust in every word that came from the mouth of God. The enemy caused them to doubt the truth, and thereby shift their loyalties.

In the second temptation the devil had the audacity to quote scripture: "Then the devil took him to the holy city and placed him on the pinnacle of the temple, saying to him, '*If you are the Son of God*, throw yourself down; for it is written, "He will command his angels concerning you," and "On their hands they will bear you up, so that you will not dash your foot against a stone."' Jesus said to him, 'Again it is written, "Do not put the Lord your God to the test"'" (Matthew 4:5–7, NRSV, emphasis added). Immediately Jesus rejected this interpretation of the Old Testament psalm and the way the enemy was trying to distort the truth. Using his own interpretation of Scripture, the enemy was trying to "incite distrust in the faithfulness of God."[29] Jesus saw through the tactics of Satan and will "not put God to the test as his ancestors did at Massah and Meribah."[30]

29. Robert S. Snow and Arseny Ermakov, *Matthew: A Commentary in the Wesleyan Tradition, New Beacon Bible Commentary* (Kansas City: The Foundry Publishing, 2019), 83.
30. Snow and Ermakov, *Matthew*, 83.

True identity is a threat to the enemy's power. This is why the enemy will distort the Word of God and tantalize humanity with the lure of other identities that are not found in our relationship to God. To accept the lie results in a loss of freedom. When we reach out and embrace the new identity handed to us by the enemy, we are left worshipping a golden calf. Having watched our true identity in Christ slip through our fingers, the enemy holds us hostage to the identity we have chosen to embrace.

As children of God, we are to live in truth and this is a lifelong journey. In his Nobel Prize acceptance speech, Albert Camus said, "Truth is mysterious, elusive, ever to be won anew. Liberty is dangerous, as hard to get along with as it is exciting. We must progress toward those two objectives, painfully but resolutely, sure in advance that we shall weaken and flinch on such a long road."[31] The journey toward truth as God's children is worth the price that we must pay if we are to live in glorious freedom, for only in the freedom we have in Christ can our true identity be revealed.

Jesus remained victorious over the temptations that he faced and, as a result, was able to maintain his identity as the Son of God and offer us the invitation to live as children of the king. This gift brings with it a complete paradigm shift as we learn to live free from the shackles of the identities that may be placed on us, and we learn to live in our primary identity as God's child. While Jesus remained firm in the face of temptation, the Israelites did not. Over and over again they succumbed to temptation, failing to live in the power that was offered to them as God's people. Along the way, however,

31. Albert Camus, in his acceptance speech upon being awarded the Nobel Prize for Literature, December 10, 1957. Accessed Feb. 24, 2020, https://uuwestport.org/albert-camus-from-his-nobel-prize-acceptance-speech/.

one man always seemed to be able to live above fray and this was Moses. Something was different about him and the way he carried himself.

Maybe the way Moses carried himself had something to do with the way he had been raised. While everyone else in the Israelite community had been raised as a slave, Moses had not. Therefore, he was a Hebrew, but one who had been raised by Pharaoh's daughter in the household of the ruler of the land. He "was educated in all the wisdom of the Egyptians and"—while having a fear of speaking publicly—"was powerful in speech and action" (Acts 7:22). Moses was raised as a member of the dominant culture of his time. There came a moment when he realized his true identity as a Jew and decided to defend "his people," but the Israelites viewed him with suspicion because, to them, he still represented the Egyptians (Exodus 2:11–14).

While Moses may have felt confused, we begin to see that God had a plan for all of these experiences. Moses had to be raised in Pharaoh's house so he would not have a slave mentality. A leader who is in slavery internally cannot free those who are in slavery externally. The Lord needed someone who could stand face to face with Pharaoh and speak with boldness and dignity in order to free the Israelites from slavery. This is why God prepared Moses, who was raised and educated as a king and had never been a slave, but was broken enough to be used in a mighty way.

Moses went through a period of time when he seemed to be confused about his identity and where he was supposed to fit in the world. He fled to the land of Midian, where he married a woman and settled down as a shepherd. One day, while Moses was caring for his father-in-law's sheep, God called out to him. The man who stood before the burning bush was yearning for a new identity, one that would reach beyond his

Hebrew culture (the dominated culture) and the opposing culture of his adopted Egypt (the dominant culture).

We find a debate in the Scriptures that characterizes a search for identity. Moses asked God, "Who am I that I should go to Pharaoh, and bring the Israelites out of Egypt?" (Exodus 3:11, NRSV). Moses had yet to realize who he really was, for he was living with a loss of identity. He was no longer Pharaoh's son, nor was he embraced as the son of his biological mother. Moses was a foreigner living in a foreign land—a man who had lost any tie to his identity. But this was why God could use him, for God was about to reveal to him his true identity, and this, in relation to God alone.

As a promise that his identity was to be found in God, the Lord said, "I will be with you" (v. 12, NRSV). When we are wrapped up in the identity that we are given from God, we can be assured of God's presence. And yet, Moses still had doubts and asked God to reveal his name. This is a significant moment because, for the first time in history the God of all creation shared his name with his people: "God said to Moses, 'I AM WHO I AM'" (v. 14, NRSV). He told Moses to remind the Israelites, "I AM has sent me to you."

This I AM is the "God of Abraham, the God of Isaac, and the God of Jacob" (v. 15, NRSV). Identity is being revealed, the relationship is clear, and now the family name is shared. No longer is there any confusion regarding identity, but Moses can live freely as one of God's children.

In one of the more poignant episodes of Moses's walk with God, we see his new identity as a friend, a confidante, and a child of God. We find Moses standing before God and saying, "Why should your anger burn against your people, whom you brought out of Egypt with great power and a mighty hand? Why should the Egyptians say, ' . . . Remember your servants

Abraham, Isaac, and Israel, to whom you swore by your own self: "I will make your descendants as numerous as the stars in the sky and I will give your descendants all this land I promised them, and it will be their inheritance forever'"" (Exodus 32:11–13). Moses was now confident enough in his identity as a child of God to have an honest conversation about his concerns.

Once Moses found his identity in his relationship with God, he was able to live free from personal ambition. Cultural pride and his deep, inner fears disappeared because he found freedom, and this freedom was in embracing the mindset that he was the child of the king. No longer was he concerned about himself, but about the reputation of his heavenly Father. This is the mark of an authentic child of God, one whose identity has been restored, and whose language has become: "My food . . . is to do the will of him who sent me" (John 4:34). Like Jesus, Moses was born free and lived as a king. The difference is that Jesus was king by nature and he transferred the royal robes to us by adoption.

The gift from Jesus brings with it a complete paradigm shift as we learn to live free from the shackles of identity that we may have allowed to be placed on us. The enemy wants to take our true identity and steal it from us, replacing it with labels placed upon us by culture. Now, we learn to live in our primary identity as a child of the king.

God's children, the world over, are invited to embrace their true identity, which can only be found in Christ. This starts when each of us, individually, releases any identity that holds us hostage to the things of this world, and we proudly put on the purple robes of royalty, identifying ourselves as children of God's kingdom. In addition, we must be willing to examine ourselves critically and release any identities, or any dominant cultures, which may hold a brother or sister in Christ in bondage. The beauty of the kingdom is revealed when each child of God is set free to reflect the identity that they have been given as an adopted child of God. Because of Jesus this is possible for all. "So if the Son makes you free, you will be free indeed" (John 8:36, NRSV).

QUESTIONS FOR REFLECTION

1. List your different identities or ways you would describe yourself.

   _____

   _____

2. Close your eyes and imagine that you have brothers and sisters from every race in the world. What would your family look like?

   _____

   _____

3. In what ways does the world ask us to identify ourselves and what questions do they ask?

   _____

   _____

4. What does it mean for you to embrace your kingdom citizenship?

   _____

   _____

5. How can living into your identity "in Christ" give you freedom?

   _____

   _____

6

GOLD

*The Golden Thread
of Doctrine (Holiness)*

Carla and Dany

Holiness. Perfection. Purity. Sanctification. These words come to mind when we think about our holiness heritage. This doctrine, or golden thread, has come to us through many voices and has sometimes made the local fabric stronger and more beautiful, and at other times it has threatened to tear at the seams. As we sit over a cup of espresso or tea at a Mugg & Bean, the South African coffee chain, the conversation bears down on this doctrinal thread.

"Why is holiness important to us?"

"How do we define holiness, and has it been, at times, defined culturally?"

"Is there a singular definition of holiness, and what is *the* definition?"

We discover that the golden thread remains consistent, while the expressions may vary.

In Africa, we find a triad of holiness: this includes purity, peace, and power. Most of the concepts of purity were brought to Africa from the perspective of the Western church. Because the cultures were so different, the idea of purity was frequently emphasized, but with a Western mindset. This was an inward and individualistic perspective, which was foreign to the outward and communal life of the African. Legalism was the result, which felt more culturally restrictive than spiritually guided. Our differing worldviews impact how we receive the message of holiness. The view of the first world usually focuses on guilt, but this is just one aspect of the atonement. Our teaching on holiness needs to tie all three of these concepts together.

The concept of peace fits much better in African culture, which is based on honor and shame. Peace is about reconciliation and our relationship with God and others. This concept of *shalom* helps us to understand our wholeness in God. When we are in harmony with God, we are made complete, not just with God and each other, but with the cosmic world as well. This leads to an understanding of power and an authority over evil spirits. As God's children, we are invited into the heavenlies, but this is a place of spiritual warfare. Holiness brings us into a life of power. All of this brings the message of holiness alive within the African context. The thread is there, but the fabrics are slightly different.

This leads us to another question regarding perfection: "Who has been setting the standard for holiness?" Again, we have to ask whether this has been culturally defined, or whether it is by God's divine intention.

The animal parks of Africa often bring to mind the Garden of Eden. Driving through Kruger National Park and searching for the Big Five (rhino, elephant, buffalo, lion, leopard), a person can easily be in awe of God's creation. The expansive beauty of artistic work lay before God. In all its perfection, creation was still lacking one element, the one that would shine with the glorious reflection of the Creator. Therefore, God said, "'Let us make humankind in our image, according to our likeness; and let them have dominion over the fish of the sea, and over the birds of the air, and over the cattle, and over all the wild animals of the earth, and over every creeping thing that creeps upon the earth.' So God created humankind in his image, in the image of God he created them; male and female he created them" (Genesis 1:26–27, NRSV). Suddenly, there they were in the garden, absolute perfection, radiating the glory of God for all the world to see.

It's in this beginning that we see the end; that which they were from the beginning is what humanity is intended to become again. Humanity is perfection when the golden glory of God is reflected in the lives of those who seek God's face. And this is for all of humanity.

Searching the end, we then find the beginning, and the hope for all of humanity. In John's Revelation of Jesus Christ, we discover a conversation about a rod of gold and the need to measure the work that has been done:

The angel who talked to me had a measuring rod of gold to measure the city and its gates and walls. The city lies four-square, its length the same as its width; and he measured the city with his rod, fifteen hundred miles; its length and width and height are equal. He also measured its wall, one hundred forty-four cubits by human measurement, which the angel was using. The wall is built of jasper, while the city is pure gold, clear as glass. The foundations of the wall of the city are adorned with every jewel; the first was jasper, the second sapphire, the third agate, the fourth emerald, the fifth onyx, the sixth carnelian, the seventh chrysolite, the eighth beryl, the ninth topaz, the tenth chrysoprase, the eleventh jacinth, the twelfth amethyst. And the twelve gates are twelve pearls, each of the gates is a single pearl, and the street of the city is pure gold, transparent as glass.

(Revelation 21:15-21, NRSV)

Oddly enough, we might wonder why it's necessary to have an angel measure the city, its gates, and walls, if God has created all of this. Back up just a few scenes and we discover that this moment of measurement is in contrast to what was happening in chapter 11. There is no angel in the earlier scene, just John, who is measuring. He was handed a rod and the purpose of his measuring had to do with ensuring the defense of the people. John, the human, was measuring for the purpose of protection.

Back to the current scene and the situation has changed. The angel has now come to measure the city of God. The angel has a rod of gold with which to measure the city, ensuring the city's integrity and purity. This angel will measure the gates and the height of the walls, revealing the enormity of the city, but also the perfect symmetry. This city is to become the dwelling place of the faithful for all of eternity, for those who are reflecting the image of the Creator.

Day in and day out, we are influenced by those around us. In many ways, we allow ourselves to be measured by those from whom we want to receive acceptance or affirmation. The dominant culture speaks to us. Recently, while shopping in the United Kingdom we saw a chart that was designed to help us understand the different ways you can measure jeans. It was a scale, in the form of a measuring stick, where you could find yourself on the jeans continuum. It included the following increments: spray-on, super skinny, skinny, slim, tapered, straight, bootcut. Can you imagine, in some economy we are being measured by the tightness of our jeans! There are measures that we allow into our lives, and by these we somehow think we can discover how we fit into the world.

John's measurements were being taken in the human realm. They had to do with measuring up to the world's power, strength, and influence. Many of us are caught with the rod of iron in our hands, wishing desperately to be accepted by those around us. The angel came to measure something different. This measurement had everything to do with the spiritual realm, for this rod was to reveal perfection.

That word *perfection* grabs our attention, for it means something in particular to those within the holiness tradition. Perfection, in the spiritual sense, is to fulfill the purpose for which you have been created, and that is to be God's holy people. At the same time, each of us has been uniquely and beautifully crafted at the hands of the Creator, who knows the intimate details of every design and purpose. Just like artists hold within themselves the criteria for their own paintings, so our heavenly Father knows the potential for beauty within every one of his creations.

This understanding must then beg the question, "How are you being measured?" When we turn from the measures of this world and focus upon the golden rod of God, we will discover how we are doing in life. God's measure is far different from that of the world, and it's only by the Lord's measure that we will find the place of spiritual symmetry: a place where we can learn to trust and rest for all of time.

But now, let's consider this question of measurement in relation to God's church. Maybe we find ourselves somewhere in this vision of measurement. We create standards and measures we consider normal, but in reality, they may simply be the rod in John's hand. This is a protective rod, one that is afraid of change and of anything that may exist outside of our control. This is the rod of the dominant culture.

Enter God's rod of gold. What if we are supposed to embrace the rod that measures perfection in relation to the Creator? Every one of us has been created with unique giftings and abilities. No two people will ever pastor a church the same way or worship the Lord in the same manner, and yet, we stand next to the human measuring stick and wonder how we measure up! We create an iron rod of measurement for a healthy church in the northern hemisphere and then place that rod next to a church in an entirely different environment and determine that they don't measure up.

What happens when we embrace the rod of protection, rather than the rod of perfection? We miss out on radiating the glory of God's image in our lives. The rod of perfection allows the glorious beauty of God's creation to shine in this world.

Throughout God's story, we are reminded that we are to reflect the glory of God. We find individuals on their spiritual journey who provide roadmaps of discovery, revealing humanity in desperate desire to return to the original image of God. We find Moses climbing the mountain to be in the presence of God, his heart so directed toward his Creator that he desires nothing more than to see God's glory. As Moses returns down the mountain, the people are overwhelmed by God's radiant glory reflected in his face. They cry out for him to cover his face with a veil, unwilling to live in the life laid out before them by a holy and loving God.

Later we discover David, overwhelmed by his circumstances, surrounded by the enemy. What did he do? He looked to God to deliver him: "I sought the LORD, and he answered me, and delivered me from all my fears. Look to him, and be radiant; so your faces shall never be ashamed. This poor soul cried, and was heard by the LORD, and was saved from every trouble. The angel of the LORD encamps around those who fear him, and delivers them" (Psalm 34:4–7, NRSV). He turned toward the God that he knew loved him and would care for him in the midst of his deepest need. As he looked to God, his face radiated with the glory of God's presence. God heard his cries and rescued him in the midst of his difficult situation.

Moving to the New Testament, we find Jesus settling in to preach his Sermon on the Mount. The people from across the region fill the hillside, eager to hear his words. We listen in as he encourages those listening: "You are the light of the world. A city built on a hill cannot be hid. No one after lighting a lamp puts it under the bushel basket, but on the lampstand, and it gives light to all in the house. In the same way, let your light shine before others, so that they may see your good works and give glory to your Father in heaven" (Matthew 5:14–16, NRSV).

Jesus is talking about light and that his disciples are to be the light! The people ask, "How do we become the light?" The answer comes from the beginning and leads to the end. The light is from God alone, and again, we must seek the face of God, and in this way, we become his light to the world. It is his radiant glory that lights up the world, and this is the light that no one can hide.

God's radiant and golden glory has always represented God's presence. God's people, restored in his image, reflect his image and his glorious presence. No matter where we find ourselves in the world, this is possible, for this is the golden thread that ties everything together. Just as Moses was radiant after coming down from the mountain, so Peter, James, and John experienced firsthand the radiance of God's holy presence on the Mount of Transfiguration. David knew that he desperately needed help from the Father and, therefore, he settled into God's holy presence, relaxing in the grace of God. All of these understood that the beginning led to the end. God's people, all of them, are continually invited into a relationship where they find fellowship with the Creator.

Just as the closing chapters of Revelation bring us to what is most important, so we turn the page on the past and allow God to become our measuring rod. There is no reason to compare ourselves with others, by the dominant culture, or by the standards of this world. That will only lead to frustration because the world is not our Creator, and if we depend upon the world's imperfect measuring rod, we will be found wanting. God's good measure will bring us a level of peace, or *shalom*, that cannot be found in the measurements of this world.

Embracing the golden rod, the glory of God is revealed in us individually and corporately. This restores God's intention for all of humanity, for this is God's divine perfection, and we have the incredible privilege of participating in this mission.

Holiness. Perfection. Purity. Peace. Power. "The angel who talked to me had a measuring rod of gold" (Revelation 21:15, NRSV).

QUESTIONS FOR REFLECTION

1. Why would the triad of purity, peace, and power be help-ful to your understanding of holiness?

_____

_____

_____

2. Where have you gotten your standard for holiness?

_____

_____

_____

3. How would you describe the dominant culture in your life?

_____

_____

_____

4. What do you think about God's peace, or *shalom*, being a part of the holy life? How is that experienced?

_____

_____

_____

7

RED

Spiritual Warfare

Dany and Carla

"They sing a new song: 'You are worthy to take the scroll and to open its seals, for you were slaughtered and by your blood you ransomed for God saints from every tribe and language and people and nation.'"

—*Revelation 5:9, NRSV*

The water glistened in the sunlight of a cloudless sky as we crossed the Atlantic Ocean. The shoreline of Guinea Bissau became a sliver across the horizon with nothing but water in our sights, and we prayed that the captain of our boat knew where we were going. It was a day of great anticipation as nearly twenty young people, living on a small island, were awaiting their baptism, ready to embrace their newfound faith in Jesus Christ. Following Jesus would not be easy in a community populated by witch doctors who were unhappy with the turn of events in their village. Public baptism was an invitation to participate in spiritual warfare.

Images of war are never pleasant, and the thought of engaging in battle can be frightening. Sometimes it's simply easier to close our eyes and try to remain blissfully ignorant of the storms brewing around us. Western culture tries to produce rational explanations and creates a spirit/material world dichotomy, while the African world is prone to see a spirit hiding behind every rock and tree with no explanation but the supernatural.

Somewhere between these two, potentially polar-opposite worldviews, we suddenly find ourselves on common ground because the enemy has learned to deceive each of us in our own territory. Years ago, Dr. Paul Orjala said that the devil changes according to every environment: If he's in a place where they think he doesn't exist, he will dress in a suit and look civilized, while in some parts of Africa, he will morph into the psyche of the people and pursue them at their level of understanding. The enemy is doing battle in every culture, society, and country of this world.

In the Gospel of Mark, we find Jesus taking the disciples on a journey throughout the region of Galilee. Jesus's ministry of preaching, healing, and teaching came to a climax when he challenged the disciples by asking them, "But who do you say that I am?" He had been revealing himself to them through every action and word, and now it was essential for them to recognize him and his authority.

This gospel becomes critical for the church in Africa, where most people see evil spirits behind every bush and seek for specific prayers for each of their fears and beliefs inherited from their animist background. The Gospel of Mark gradually demonstrates Jesus's authority over every fear of the African, because his ministry was centered around the realities of these fears: he cast out demons (fear of evil spirits), he healed every sickness (fear of inherited illnesses), he rejected the common belief in family curses, he calmed the storm (fear of spirits in the nature), he walked on the water (fear of water spirits), he resurrected a dead person (fear of dead people and ancestors' spirits). Above all, Jesus gave complete healing to people (blind, lepers, the demon possessed, deaf man, etc.). In this way Jesus demonstrated that he gives Africans the "harmony" they need by becoming true worshippers in spirit and in truth (John 4:23). Jesus knew that all of this had been revealed to his disciples, but until they could answer the pivotal question regarding his identity, they could go no further, for they must be able to trust in his power and authority to overcome all that they would encounter in the days ahead.

There is no value in speaking about spiritual warfare if we do not believe that Christ has the power and authority to destroy sin. When our evangelistic efforts focus only on the forgiveness of sin, a vacuum is created in the lives of believers who need to be freed from the fear of death, demons, and Satan. Because Jesus entered into the human experience, he took on the battle for us, defeating every enemy and offering us complete freedom. The clash of cultures comes when the analytical meets the spirit-driven mind. For far too long, Western missionaries to Africa rarely mentioned the victory of Christ over Satan, even though this is the ever-present worldview in the life of Africans. Embracing a "Christ as Victor" paradigm leads us to see that Jesus has victory over the powers that hold people in bondage, including sin, death, and the devil. Jesus's victory brings the rule of these fears to an end and sets all of humanity free from their dominion.[32] The doctrinal thread of sanctification leads us to this conclusion, "that Christ came to destroy the principle of lawlessness which was the devil's chief work in humankind."[33]

Again, different perspectives lead us to diverse understandings of Christ's victory. In Western culture, there tends to be a greater focus on the individual rather than the community. When speaking about Christ's victory, some cultures embrace an emphasis on the inward victory over sin. This means that victory can be experienced in the personal life over the temptations that may be faced. Compare this to living in a community that embraces the concept of *Ubuntu*, a Nguni Bantu term that refers to humanity. Trying to translate the term is difficult but the concept is often expressed as, "I am because we are." Suddenly, Christ's victory over Satan becomes much more important because the enemy may attack the entire community, not just an individual. Jesus is the Victor over the powers and the forces that hold our communities hostage.

Madam Afua Kuma, a farmer in the forest of Ghana, invites us into this understanding through her prayer:

If Satan troubles us,
Jesus Christ,
You who are the Lion of the grasslands,
You whose claws are sharp,
Will tear out his entrails,
And leave them on the ground
For the flies to eat.
Let us all say, Amen![34]

---

32. Gustaf Aulen, *Christus Victor* (Austin, TX: Wise Path Books, 2016), 20.

33. William H. Greathouse, "Sanctification and the *Christus Victor* Motif," *Africa Speaks: An Anthology of the Africa Nazarene Theology Conference 2003* (South Africa: Africa Nazarene Publications, 2004), 14.

34. Afua Kuma, *Jesus of the Deep Forest: Prayers and Praises of Afua Kuma* (Accra, Ghana: Asempa Publishers, 1981), 46.

We return again to the Gospel of Mark where shortly after Peter's declaration of Christ as the Messiah, Jesus took him, along with James and John, to the top of a high mountain. There Jesus was transfigured before their eyes; a moment when human nature met God and they were able to bear witness to the unique character of Christ. Entering history, Jesus met the forces of evil on their territory so he could break their power. "Since, therefore, the children share flesh and blood, he himself likewise shared the same things, so that through death he might destroy the one who has the power of death, that is, the devil, and free those who all their lives were held in slavery by the fear of death" (Hebrews 2:14–15, NRSV). Their understanding of the power in Christ grows moment by moment, while revealing that Jesus became what we are so that we might become what he is!

In the first century there was no New Testament, and very few people had access to read the Torah. Many people, especially the gentiles, were illiterate when it came the Holy Scriptures, so discipleship became the key. The apostle Paul wrote letters to his churches, encouraging the people and congregations to continue to grow spiritually. Paul embraced the life of Jesus Christ, wanting to know him intimately. He talked of straining toward the goal, and allowed his own life to be used as a model for others. In his role as mentor and guide, he wrote to the church in Corinth, "Be imitators of me, as I am of Christ" (1 Corinthians 11:1, NRSV).

Lifting up Jesus Christ empowers the individual and the body of Christ. Through Christ's life and death, there is victory over the internal and external forces of evil. We are able to face those forces because Christ is in us and because we take seriously the challenge to imitate him.

One of the African languages uses two distinct words for "imitation": *topondo* and *rooy*. The first word, *topondo*, usually means mimicking, repeating the actions, words, or manners of someone. This is just like the parrot and the monkey imitating what they see, or hearing without even knowing or caring about the essence of their words or actions. In spiritual warfare, one of the major weapons of the enemy is imitation, for he is the great imitator. The Lord Jesus warns us about the imitators: "At that time if anyone says to you, 'Look, here is the Messiah!' or, 'There he is!' do not believe it. For false messiahs and false prophets will appear and perform great signs and wonders to deceive, if possible, even the elect" (Matthew 24:23–24). At the end of times there will be many false prophets, wolves in sheep's clothing. They are like the monkey; they do things for people to like them and to fear them more than they fear God. Their identity is no longer found in Jesus the Lord, but in a simple man or woman whom they are serving. *There is nothing that makes you more powerless and vulnerable than when your identity is taken from you.*

In contrast, the apostle Paul is calling people to imitate (*rooy*) him as he is imitating the Lord Jesus. The second African word, *rooy*, is about looking at the character of the person and trying to reproduce it in your own life. Paul's source of being is rooted in the person and work of Jesus. As Dany's friend Fred Hartley from the College of Prayer International rightly said, "Apart from Christ, the strongest person is weaker than the weakest demon; but the weakest person in Christ is stronger than the strongest demon."

Pastoring in Africa has its challenges. I, Dany, have had the privilege of serving for more than twenty years in West Africa and watching God work in supernatural ways. Several years ago, a pastor friend and I experienced this truth in a very dramatic way. We went to visit one of our church members, and when we arrived, she was sitting with her mother and her sister. We started to share about the Word of God with them, and her sister, who was not a believer but was very open, decided to give her life to the Lord. We were so excited that I started to speak to the mother, telling her that she was the cause of most of the bad issues happening in her family, and I urged her to leave her evil practices and involvement in divination. All of a sudden, she stood and started insulting us while her voice and face changed.

My pastor friend and I spent the next three hours trying to deliver her without success. She had formidable strength and was becoming more and more threatening, until at one point, when suddenly, I seemed to hear a quiet voice telling me that we should both kneel down. I was not sure that was a good idea because it was a position of vulnerability before this threatening woman. However, I told my friend what I had heard, and we knelt and continued to pray with our eyes closed. Suddenly, she started to shout, "They are coming! They are coming!" and we heard a great noise as if the floor were shaking. When we opened our eyes, we saw her lying, with her arms opened, as if she were dead. A few minutes later, she came back to her senses and said, "When you knelt, I saw a group of angels coming with power, and it knocked me down."

We experienced what the apostle Paul described in one of the most powerful illustrations of the victory of Jesus on the cross: "And having disarmed the powers and authorities, he made a public spectacle of them, triumphing over them by the cross" (Colossians 2:15). When Jesus died on the cross and shed his blood, he disarmed all powers and authorities. In doing so, he set the people free. This disarming uncovered the powers and authorities, revealing their deception and leaving them naked, exposed, and powerless. Jesus was breaking down the lies and exposing the evil one for having taken authority, stripping him of all power. The enemy and all other powers and authorities were paraded as prisoners of war, as Jesus revealed their true identity. This is what happened in the spiritual world while Jesus was on the cross, defeating all other powers and authorities.

The world deceives, saying that it was Jesus on the cross who was naked, exposed, and powerless, but this is the great lie. The onlookers could only see a man hanging on a cross, but there was so much more that was going on. In the spiritual world, it was a much different view, and when it was over, on the third day, he rose from the dead. But before that, he said, "It is finished." It has come to completion.

The enemy is defeated. Flesh is defeated. The world is defeated.

The veil of the temple tore open for people to see that they could enter, because the work was finished. The invitation stands for us all to now come and follow Jesus and enter his presence. Yes, "the Son of Man came to seek and to save the lost" (Luke 19:10), but also "the reason the Son of God appeared was to destroy the devil's work" (1 John 3:8). Jesus Christ, the Son of God, has set us free, "It is for freedom that Christ has set us free. Stand firm, then, and do not let yourselves be burdened again by a yoke of slavery" (Galatians 5:1). It is one thing to be free, it is another one to stand firm in your freedom and live in that freedom, day after day.

Imitation of Christ includes a study of the ways he lived out his life in daily contact with the Father. Jesus showed us the need to pray, and therefore, our imitation of Christ—our ability to stand firm in his power and authority—is through prayer.

Far too often, we think that prayer is about bringing our needs before God—which is partially true—but prayer is more of a place, one in which there is intimate contact with the Lord. Through prayer we "become partakers of the divine nature" (2

Peter 1:4, ESV). This is where we discover the source of power. We have no power on our own, but by participating with God, we take on the power that Jesus revealed on the cross.

Our leadership across Africa is encouraged to stand in the freedom found in Christ by praying daily for protection, direction, and revelation. What a beautiful model for a church that reaches beyond culture and embraces the wholeness of life to be found in Christ. We pray for *protection*, asking God our Father to cover us with his wings as we begin our day. Then, we move into *direction*, asking our Lord Jesus, the Good Shepherd, to show us the path forward. If we follow, the Lord will guide. Finally, we pray for *revelation*, asking the Holy Spirit to provide wisdom and inspiration as God is continually revealed.

As we've said before, throughout the Gospel of Mark we see the authority of Christ revealed. We also see the disciples, on more than one occasion, in a boat, out on the sea. The sea becomes a metaphor for the world around us, while the boat is a vision of the church. The disciples knew the sea very well, for it was the world in which they had been raised. Many of them were fishermen who had spent hours in the boat and on the water, skillfully navigating the sea from a very young age. And yet, we see the waters churning as Jesus moved from shore to shore to engage in spiritual battles. Those who should have been sure of themselves became terrified and feared for their lives while Jesus calmly slept on the cushion.

Jesus was never afraid of the world that would rock the boat, or the church, because he knew that he had ultimate power and authority. Jesus lived, died, and was resurrected in victory. He invites us to participate in his victory as we continue on our spiritual climb in the faith. For us to embrace his victory, we are to continually exalt the name of Jesus. All of the victory is his, and any time that we deviate, or begin to claim anything on the human side, we will find ourselves in trouble. We will join Peter, sinking in the water! Exalt Jesus first thing in the morning. Wake up and proclaim, "Jesus is Lord!" We must be worshippers of the Lord on high.

Not only do we embrace a life of worship, but we also live in holiness. This is again, the golden thread that holds everything together. The holiness of Jesus is to be reflected in how we live and the ethical decisions we make every day. A Christ follower who does not reflect or imitate Christ is a powerless disciple. The Spirit-filled life brings victory, and the result is a daily walk filled with holiness and power.

Finally, we are encouraged to put on the full armor of God. Paul knew the power that would be found in a church that displayed the beauty of God found in diversity. He also seemed to understand that this would be challenging and would draw out forces that would seek to bring division:

> Finally, be strong in the Lord and in the strength of his power. Put on the whole armor of God, so that you may be able to stand against the wiles of the devil. For our struggle is not against enemies of blood and flesh, but against the rulers, against the authorities, against the cosmic powers of this present darkness, against the spiritual forces of evil in the heavenly places. Therefore take up the whole armor of God, so that you may be able to withstand on that evil day, and having done everything, to stand firm. Stand therefore, and fasten the belt of truth around your waist, and put on the breastplate of righteousness. As shoes for your feet put on whatever will make you ready to proclaim the gospel of peace. With all of these, take the shield of faith, with which you will be able to quench all the flaming arrows of the evil one. Take the helmet of salvation, and the sword of the Spirit, which is the word of God.
>
> (Ephesians 6:10–17, NRSV)

Praying on the armor of God every day can bring power and protection. Daily, we are to wear the armor of God as we live in this world. Put on the belt of truth, for Jesus is Truth. Live the holy life as you wear the breastplate of righteousness. Never forget to put on the shoes that will lead you into places where you can share the good news of Jesus. Carry the shield of faith, firmly holding onto belief in Jesus Christ, trusting in the helmet of salvation to lead into new life, and study the Word of God so that the power of Christ is at your fingertips. The Jesus whom we serve is the same yesterday, today, and forever.

Let's return to one of the storm scenes in Mark:

> On that day, when evening had come, he said to them, "Let us go across to the other side." And leaving the crowd behind, they took him with them in the boat, just as he was. Other boats were with him. A great windstorm arose, and the waves beat into the boat, so that the boat was already being swamped. But he was in the stern, asleep on the cushion; and they woke him up and said to him, "Teacher, do you not care that we are perishing?" He woke up and rebuked the wind, and said to the sea, "Peace! Be still!" Then the wind ceased, and there was a dead calm. He said to them, "Why are you afraid? Have you still no faith?" And they were filled with great awe and said to one another, "Who then is this, that even the wind and the sea obey him?"
>
> (Mark 4:35–41, NRSV)

The description of the storm is vivid. If Mark is repeating Peter's firsthand account, then we have an idea of how bad this situation was. Sudden storms are not uncommon on the Sea of Galilee, where the wind can come down off of the surrounding heights, especially late in the day or early evening. This wind came, almost with tornadic force, and the boat was swamped by waves. These big, strong, professional fishermen were suddenly terrified. They awakened the carpenter rabbi who was exhausted and had fallen fast asleep. Their experience with Jesus meant they had developed a faith that led them to believe that awakening him would make a difference. They were beginning to understand the need for the shield of faith.

It appears that the disciples scolded Jesus when he got up and rebuked nature. The disciples—all of them; not just those in the boat with him, but in the other surrounding boats—were stunned. Everyone was looking in awe at Jesus, who had suddenly stilled the storm. The disciples found themselves in silence on the sea.

Jesus revealed that he had authority over the wind and the waves. The metaphor speaks to us from across the centuries, for the disciples were going to experience rough water in their day. They would become the persecuted church at the hands of the Roman Empire, trying to keep the boat upright in the raging world of chaos. Jesus's power is revealed to be greater than nature, the chaos of this world, and anything that the enemy can throw our way. Kent Brower puts it this way, "Jesus's sleep is probably due to exhaustion. Perhaps, as a part of the conflict with evil in which he is engaged, the storm arises because he is in the boat. If so, the storm is symbolic of opposition to God and his rule. In this context, his mastery over the sea and the storm appear to be important for the subsequent story."[35] The subsequent story is the healing of Legion.

In the West, we try to explain away some of Jesus's miracles or confrontations with evil, not as demoniacs, but as those suffering from seizures or mental illness. But how do we explain this miracle over nature? Mark uses this moment to

---

35. Kent Brower, *Mark: A Commentary in the Wesleyan Tradition, New Beacon Bible Commentary* (Kansas City: Beacon Hill Press of Kansas City, 2012), 139–40.

speak beyond culture, for before Jesus could engage in other miracles, he demonstrated that his power was far greater than the disciples could imagine. His power cannot be explained by human standards, but is supernatural.

Augustine, an early church father from North Africa, provides us with an interesting application of this passage:

> When you have to listen to abuse, that means you are being buffeted by the wind. When your anger is roused, you are being tossed by the waves. So when the winds blow and the waves mount high, the boat is in danger, your heart is imperiled, your heart is taking a battering. On hearing yourself insulted, you long to retaliate; but the joy of revenge brings with it another kind of misfortune—shipwreck. Why is this? Because Christ is asleep in you. What do I mean? I mean you have forgotten his presence. Rouse him, then; remember him, let him keep watch within you, pay heed to him. . . . A temptation arises: it is the wind. It disturbs you: it is the surging of the sea. This is the moment to awaken Christ and let him remind you of those words: "Who can this be? Even the winds and the sea obey him."[36]

With Jesus in the boat, his power is revealed, and it is much more than what meets the eye. Whether we find ourselves in a metaphorical storm, or a real one, we need to open our eyes to see the power of God. Far too often we create the limits or boundaries for God's activity in this world because of our own fears. David Garland tells us that Jesus's "sleep during the storm contrasts with the disciples' terror. God 'grants sleep to those he loves' (Psalm 127:2), and Jesus's sleep reflects his serene trust in God, who watches over him."[37]

---

36. Augustine, Sermons 63.1–3.
37. ZIBBCNT-26, Clinton E. Arnold, General Editor, Electronic Edition Oak Tree Software, David Garland on Mark.

Reflecting upon who Christ really is must be central to spiritual warfare. Looking beyond the material, we discover the transcendent God who is able to do much more than we can ever ask or imagine, for far too often in life there are circumstances that are beyond our understanding.

Back on the island in West Africa, we completed our visit where the young people had been baptized. The excitement of getting to know Jesus had been evident on the faces of those who were publicly declaring their faith. The last person was a young man who asked everyone to stop singing then publicly proclaimed: "So faith comes from what is heard, and what is heard comes through the word of Christ" (Romans 10:17, NRSV).

He then shouted his declaration of belief in Jesus Christ, made his way out into the water, and was baptized into new life. It felt like a Cornelius moment, an experience where those who had not known were now coming to Christ. At the same time there were those standing in the shadows, those who worship the powers of evil, who were not pleased.

As we began our return trip, the waters around us began to swirl. They looked turbulent and troubled and the waves continued to grow in size. Our missionary, who had taken this journey every month, said he'd never seen anything like it and wondered whether the enemy was displeased with the activity of the day. The boat had to slow to nearly a crawl as the captain navigated the waters. A ninety-minute trip ultimately took more than three hours, reaching shore just before sundown. Silence enveloped the group for long periods, and much prayer ensued. As the entire team, drenched from the waves, climbed from the boat, there was a realization that God's ways were much higher than our ways. While we may have been praying for the waves to calm, we discovered that our captain was deftly using the waves to surf them to shore.

What we thought was troubling, he saw as empowering and enabling. It all had to do with perspective.

The entire group testified to a deep sense of peace as we rode the waves. That is what God is asking from all of us—to trust in the Lord in the most difficult of times. God's ways are much higher than ours, and even the storms can be a blessing, if we learn that Jesus is the focus, that he has already won the victory, that we must imitate him, spend time in prayer, and live each day clothed in his armor. This is where we find power. "There is no fear in love, but perfect love casts out fear" (1 John 4:18, NRSV).

QUESTIONS FOR REFLECTION

1. How does the discussion on spiritual warfare make you feel?

_____

_____

_____

2. How does focusing on the power and authority of Christ affect the way you think about spiritual warfare?

_____

_____

_____

3. If the enemy's chief work is lawlessness, how does Christ's power and authority come into play?

_____

_____

_____

4. What does imitation of Christ look like in your own life?

_____

_____

_____

5. What does it look like for you to stand firm in your freedom?

_____

_____

_____

6. Practice praying on the full armor of God for a week, and then reflect on how that may touch your life.

_____

_____

_____

8

BLUE

Spiritual Formation, Part 1

Dany and Carla

Sometimes the student becomes the teacher. Years ago, Dany traveled from Dakar, Senegal, to Kansas City in the United States to take a class on spiritual formation at Nazarene Theological Seminary. His teacher was Carla. Little did they know that years later their paths would again cross in ministry. This time, as they traveled the continent of Africa, they were able to reflect upon the journey of faith, but now, the student would become the teacher.

In the darkness of the early morning hours, we had traveled to the airport in Dakar, Senegal, making a connection through Lagos, arriving in time for the evening traffic of Port Harcourt, Nigeria. After winding through the busy streets, we were delivered to our hotel, but too late to make it to the service on time. Not to be dissuaded, the district superintendent was awaiting our arrival and had made sure a seamstress was present. Why a seamstress? Because they wanted us—Carla and Dany's wife, Anelie—to be dressed like the other women present, so we would feel like we were a part of the community. Measurements were taken and the next morning, new dresses appeared!

Wearing these new dresses, we arrived at the gathering, where we were lovingly greeted and welcomed into the church community in Nigeria. The garments signified that we were included and that we were now a part of this beautiful community of faith.

The garments that we wear often say something about who we are and our character. In Peter's second epistle, we see that the people of God are to be intentional about their garments. In the Wolof language of Senegal this text tells us that we are to be clothed in the character of God.

> His divine power has given us everything needed for life and godliness, through the knowledge of him who called us by his own glory and goodness. Thus he has given us, through these things, his precious and very great promises, so that through them you may escape from the corruption that is in the world because of lust, and may become participants of the divine nature. For this very reason, you must make every effort to support your faith with goodness, and goodness with knowledge, and knowledge with self-control, and self-control with endurance, and endurance with godliness, and godliness with mutual affection, and mutual affection with love. For if these things are yours and are increasing among you, they keep you from being ineffective and unfruitful in the knowledge of our Lord Jesus Christ.
>
> (2 Peter 1:3-8, NRSV)

God's children are called to be effective and fruitful servants of God, no matter where they find themselves in the world.

Have you ever watched the flame on a gas stove? The color of the flame can vary from yellow to orange to red or blue. Certain types of gases burn blue while wood, coal, or candles will burn yellow, orange, or red. Interestingly, if your gas stove is not burning blue, it has a problem, because blue is a sign of complete combustion. Complete combustion occurs when there is an excellent air supply and the flame can burn extremely hot, leaving no soot or ash.[38]

Our spiritual lives are to burn blue. This is a life that is fed by the oxygen of the Holy Spirit, allowing for complete and total submission to the will of God, reflecting Christ so completely that there is no residue of sin left. No matter where we find ourselves in the world, we find that Scripture leaves us with a pattern for discipleship where the heat of the spiritual life is turned up by the presence of the Holy Spirit. The result is a disciple who is clothed in the character of God.

As we have seen throughout this book, the journey of life begins in different and varied places. Some of us were born in the country in which we currently live. Others have had to learn to adjust to new lands and cultures because of the choices made by parents. Some may have been born at home, and others in a hospital. For every one of us we begin somewhere on the journey of life and from that moment, no matter the cultural context, there is continual movement in a direction that should lead us toward God.

This movement is to be defined by the work of Jesus Christ. As we read before in Philippians 2, we are to have the same mind in us that is in Christ Jesus. This is a reflection of our participation in Christ, and through him, in the triune God.

---

38. Eric Hahn, "Blue Flame vs Yellow Flame vs Red Flame—Gas Flame Color," *LPG Gas Blog*, https://www.elgas.com.au/blog/1585-why-does-a-gas-flame-burn-blue-lpg-gas-natural-propane-methane.

This participation includes journeying throughout life with Christ, and while we are on the way, we learn about Jesus, his humility, and his self-emptying lifestyle. Coming down from the heavenly kingdom, so to speak, he was willing to move into our territory. All of this was done for our benefit, as he clothed himself in human flesh, so that he could create a way for us to be clothed in him.

The visual of this journey is easy to imagine when you're traveling across the hills of southeastern South Africa and into Eswatini (formerly Swaziland). We travel down one mountain, into the valley, and then up the next mountain. Jesus began his journey on top of the mountain but chose to come down into the valley and live with his creation. It's in the valley that he sanctifies the human journey, where every step of the ordinary life—eating, drinking, working, and resting—is made holy by his presence. Ultimately, he dies on the cross, and all of this is done so that we can be clothed in his holiness.

Jesus needs strength for the journey back up the mountain, and this comes from resurrection power. Empowered by the Holy Spirit, Jesus is able to make the journey, all the while carving out a pathway for us to follow. That's why it doesn't matter where our journey begins here on earth, because in the following of Jesus we find our spiritual way. Just as Jesus did not stay in the valley, nor are we to remain at the foot of the cross, but are to take up our cross and follow him. Following him becomes a day-by-day and step-by-step journey of faith, where we are continually growing in our faith, adding to and enriching what we have already come to understand.

The Wolof translation would encourage us to see this growth as pieces of clothing that begin to envelop not only our personal lives but also our relationships and engagement with others. When we are filled with true knowledge of Christ, then we become participants in the moral and virtuous qualities of Christ himself. We become clothed in Christ the higher we climb up the mountain. The big question for all of us is, "Will you climb the mountain?" For too many, the climb looks difficult, and so we choose to settle for second best, to remain clothed in shabby undergarments with barely any resemblance to the Christ we've been called to follow.

God's intent is that each follower would live a Christian life in which they would burn brightly for Jesus—with full combustion. This isn't something that God asks us to do on our own, for we need the presence of the Holy Spirit to empower us for the journey. That's why, in Peter's epistle, he tells us that we are invited to be participants of the divine nature. This is made possible through Jesus being clothed in the flesh. If Jesus, in the flesh, is one with the triune God, then he becomes the doorway through which we can be in holy fellowship with the divine nature, "having escaped the corruption in the world" (2 Peter 1:4). We can be dressed in the character of God, because of what Christ has done, and this is just the beginning of the journey, not the goal.

The entire journey begins with faith and grows until we reach the destination of holy love. When you think about it, faith, hope, and love are Christian virtues, ones that we, as followers of Christ, are to put on as we are on our spiritual journey. The other virtues that Peter mentions are Greco-Roman ideals that are Christianized because they are bracketed at the beginning and end by faith and love; these Christian virtues surround all the others.

All of these Christian virtues, or growth in holiness, can flourish within the beauty of a variety of cultures and settings. Holiness, because it comes from Christ, transcends culture, and yet allows culture to shine through. The day after we arrived in Nigeria, the ladies were all dressed alike, but that didn't change who we were or where we were from. It did, however, unify us as women of one body, serving the Lord together. Carla was dressed like the ladies, but still had her white skin, blond hair, and inability to dance. Dany's wife, Anelie, was also wearing the same dress, and even though she was West African—she's Senegalese—she was not suddenly Nigerian. In the dress, Anelie was radiant for who she was. When we are clothed in holiness, we are not called to conformity, but to beautiful diversity in Christ.

At times, missionaries have missed the mark; they have not understood the full calling to participation in the culture. A man came to Africa to work as a missionary and studied the local language as no other missionary before him had done. His fluency in the local language amazed all those who heard him speak. One day he was invited to a wedding and came wearing poor, traditional clothing and flip-flops. Those present were horrified at his appearance because in that culture, when you dress well, you are saying that you value and honor the event. This man could speak the language fluently but somehow missed out on learning the culture and what to wear. The shoes on his feet were ones that you wore to the toilet. He could speak the language but had put on the wrong clothes.

Unfortunately, this happens too often when it comes to the life of holiness. The language and the words may be present, but the wrong clothing is worn. The words of testimony are lost in the inappropriate attire. It doesn't matter what culture you come from, Peter tells us that we are to wear the clothing of holiness, and that is put on one piece at a time as we make the spiritual climb toward God. As we are empowered by the Holy Spirit, the flame burns blue and life is transformed.

Inward transformation will always be reflected on the outside. Our spiritual clothing will be a direct reflection of the work that God is doing in the heart. If the focus is only on outward clothing, and not the inward change, the work will only be temporal. John Wesley spoke about holiness within the framework and understanding of Christ. As a result, Christian holiness for Wesley meant "having all the mind which was in Christ, enabling us to walk as Christ walked . . . loving God with all our heart, and our neighbour as ourselves."[39] This understanding drove Wesley to engage in the work of prison reform because it was the logical outcome of his spiritual journey.

Peter tells us that the foundational undergarment required for holy living is faith. Each virtue or practice of the Christian life is based on, and springs from, the previous practice. If there is no faith, there can be no holy life. It's pretty simple—and primary: we must believe and trust in God for salvation. Forces are at work trying to chip away at our faith, telling us that we should not believe in anything that hasn't gone through the scientific process. In his book *I Don't Have Enough Faith to Be an Atheist*, Norman Geisler challenges the assumption that it's hard to have faith in God and easier to have faith in humankind and scientific study.[40] He identifies the gaps in human understanding that have to be filled with faith in something, which is far beyond believing in a Creator God.

Because all of humanity has been gifted with free will, we may choose whether or not to have faith in God. C. S. Lewis expressed this idea well, writing, "There are only two kinds of people in the end: those who say to God, 'Thy will be done,'

39. Quoted in Dean E. Flemming, *Philippians: A Commentary in the Wesleyan Tradition, New Beacon Bible Commentary* (Kansas City: Beacon Hill Press of Kansas City, 2009), 174.

40. Norman L. Geisler, *I Don't Have Enough Faith to Be an Atheist* (Wheaton, IL: Crossway Publishers).

and those to whom God says, in the end, 'Thy will be done.' All that are in Hell choose it. Without that self-choice there would be no Hell. No soul that seriously and constantly desires joy will ever miss it. Those who seek find. To those who knock it is opened."[41] We may choose to have faith in Jesus Christ, the one who saves us and makes the spiritual journey possible.

Unfortunately, the increasing secularism of many cultures has taken on the role of defining truth for society. This version of truth encourages an individualistic faith in self and social systems to provide security. All of these are Western constructs and contrary to an African communal understanding of life. While this is from the secular world, these constructs are encroaching upon the social fabric of other cultures because of the dominance of this thought. Because of the imperfections of self, and the failures of society, there is increased fear and anxiety, which are the antithesis of faith. The call from God is to come and participate in a life that is built upon faith in Jesus Christ. This is the beginning point for all of God's children.

Once we have faith in Jesus, we are able to begin telling our stories. We began this book by writing our own stories, and in the process, we found that our reflection helped us to discern our own spiritual growth and development. The apostle Peter knew that storytelling was vital, writing, "But in your hearts sanctify Christ as Lord. Always be ready to make your defense to anyone who demands from you an accounting for the hope that is in you" (1 Peter 3:15, NRSV). Telling our story is vital and becomes transformational to our lives because we can only speak of the hope that is within us when we are firmly supported by the foundation of faith. Brené Brown tells us, "When we find the courage to share our experiences and the

41. C. S. Lewis, *The Great Divorce* (New York: Macmillan, 1946), 72.

compassion to hear others tell their stories, we force shame out of hiding and end the silence. When we don't reach out, we often end up in fear, blame, and disconnection."[42] That's what happens when we stop conversing and listening to each other's stories. We begin to fear one another, placing blame and disconnecting from the relationships we may have had.

The stories of the Gomis and Sunberg families are radically different. Traveling together, we had many hours to share stories. Chuck and Carla told about how they met and how God had led them in ministry to Russia. They told about the good things in life but about those that were painful as well. Dany and Anelie talked about the transitions they have gone through in life, about their families and their children. We talked about the most recent books we had read and how they were shedding light on our thinking. We laughed, we cried, we ate, and we ministered together, and this changed our relationship. Fear is replaced with trust when we reach out to share our story with those whose story is not the same as ours.

Storytelling has often had a different name in the church—testimony. Oral storytelling is more prevalent in some cultures over others. As we drove along the roads of Ghana, our leader began telling the stories of those who were coming to Christ. Across West Africa there is a movement among those who tell the story of Jesus every day as they go about their ordinary lives. As our leader spoke, it was as if the apostle Paul himself were recounting the work that God was doing, and our hearts were encouraged because now we knew a little of what he was encountering in the mission.

In early Christianity, witnesses to the work of Jesus Christ became known as *martyrs*, and in the Roman world, it often

---

42. Brené Brown, *Dare to Lead* (New York: Random House Publishing Group), 12.

meant the ultimate sacrifice. Modern martyrs exist in areas where faith in Jesus may not be present. JESUS Film Partnership teams often take their lives into their own hands as they enter areas that are hostile to Christ. Sacrificially, they go out again and again, realizing that they may never return home, willing to become martyrs for the faith. They know the necessity of bearing witness and testifying to the reality of Jesus.

Although we can each know God intimately and personally, faith usually comes to us through interaction with another human being: This may be a mother who teaches her child how to pray, a minister preaching a message of hope, or a missionary teaching about the doctrine of holiness. In the ordinary journey of life, this may be a friend telling another how they have been transformed by an encounter with Jesus. The historian Robert Wilken reminds us, "The truth that Christians confess is transmitted through other persons, through the Christian community, the church. There is no way to Christ without *martyrs*, without witnesses."[43] All of this serves to strengthen the foundation of faith.

Obstacles to faith abound and become barriers to the spiritual growth that God intends. The enemy will use every opportunity to separate us from the community of faith where we have the potential to thrive spiritually. That's why Peter told the believers to support their faith with goodness. Wesley reminds us of the vertical and horizontal nature of our faith. We are to have a deep and abiding relationship with Jesus Christ that must be reflected by the ways we act and react in this world. Stamped in the image of God, goodness resides in the heart of every human being and it should be the work

43. Robert Louis Wilken, *The Spirit of Early Christian Thought: Seeking the Face of God* (New Haven, CT: Yale University Press, 2003), 180.

of the community of faith to provide opportunities for all to participate in acts of goodness.

Goodness is not so much a piece of clothing as it is a reflection of the body itself. Goodness comes from deep within and then becomes visible on the outside. This is strength of character, a person with values who has been shaped and formed by the indwelling nature of Jesus Christ. The result is someone with integrity who has to be willing to move out of their comfort zone, speaking and acting with courage, no matter the culture.

Sometimes, we are naïvely unaware of what is happening around us and fail to see how we are to engage with the goodness of God. I, Carla, had been flying all night from Paris to Mumbai. The previous morning, I had been up before the dawn so that I could make my flight out of Moscow. It was snowing heavily, but I decided I should dress for the city of arrival rather than my city of departure. I put a pair of sandals on my feet as I went out the door, hoping I wouldn't be too cold trudging through the snow. On the way to the airport the car skidded out of control, spinning across the three lanes of highway before my friend Vladimir got the vehicle back on the road. We made it to the airport, and I boarded my plane for Paris. Arriving a little late in Paris, I had to run through the Charles de Gaulle airport to catch my flight to Mumbai. I was joining a cadre of nurses, heading to the Reynolds Memorial Hospital in Washim for a week of teaching, and then I would spend two weeks of work with other leaders from the region that would take us across the country of India. I arrived at the gate out of breath and discovered that everyone had already boarded, but there was still time for me to make it. I found my seat, made eye contact with the other team members, and settled in for the overnight journey.

Halfway through the flight the captain announced that our flight would be longer than scheduled because war had just broken out below us—the second Gulf War. We had to get out of the airspace, out of harm's way, and finally, after many hours, we landed in Mumbai. Ready for my three-week visit to India, I waited with my team members for my luggage. It never arrived. I went to the luggage counter where they confirmed that my suitcase was sitting safely in Paris. They also informed me that they were cancelling all flights because of the war and had no idea when it might arrive in India. I had three weeks ahead and no luggage. I was glad I had worn my sandals.

All of us who had no luggage were told to get into a line; that the airline would compensate us so we could get some toiletries or necessary items. A man came out with a stack of cash and all of a sudden everyone was yelling and pushing. I really didn't know what was happening, but I was near the front of the line so I held my ground and waited until it was my turn. The man handed me the equivalent of $100 U.S. as compensation for my lost luggage. I didn't have any idea what I was supposed to get or what anything cost—I only knew that I had nothing. As far as I could tell, they were giving everyone the same amount—until they ran out of money. I was leaving the arrival hall when I heard people screaming at the man behind the counter. "You only gave her the money because she's white, and now there's nothing left for us."

I was horrified. Was it true? Hadn't I gotten what the people in front of me had gotten? Should I go back in and try to return the money? I've often reflected on that experience in the Mumbai airport. After playing it back in my mind, I do think that I was given special treatment because I was white, and that angers me. In the moment, I didn't realize what was happening because my mind didn't believe that those sorts of things really happened in this world. This was injustice at a very visible level, and it hurt deep within my soul.

Goodness is reflected by the ways in which we engage with injustice. Sometimes we don't know how to respond, but if there is goodness in us, it should create a reaction that will change future responses. We begin to see injustice and respond with goodness. Throughout the Scriptures justice and goodness are often connected:

> "You shall not pervert the justice due to your poor in their lawsuits" (Exodus 23:6, NRSV).

> "Who executes justice for the orphan and the widow, and who loves the strangers, providing them food and clothing" (Deuteronomy 10:18, NRSV).

> "You must not distort justice; you must not show partiality; and you must not accept bribes, for a bribe blinds the eyes of the wise and subverts the cause of those who are in the right. Justice, and only justice, you shall pursue, so that you may live and occupy the land that the LORD your God is giving you" (Deuteronomy 16:19-20, NRSV).

> "You shall not deprive a resident alien or an orphan of justice; you shall not take a widow's garment in pledge" (Deuteronomy 24:17, NRSV).

We see goodness in the ways that we care for the poor, the orphan, the resident alien, and the widow. Showing fairness in all transactions is paramount, and we should never allow someone to go without their very basic needs.

Years ago, in what is today Turkey, there was a terrible famine. The people of the church refused to help those who were in need. During one of his sermons, the local bishop had this criticism of his congregation:

> You gorgeously array your walls, but do not clothe your fellow human being; you adorn horses, but turn away from the shameful plight of your brother or sister; you allow grain to rot in your barns, but do not feed those who are starving; you hide gold in the earth but ignore the oppressed! And if your wife happens to be a money-loving person, then the disease is doubled in its effects. She stirs up the love of luxury and inflames the craving for pleasure, spurring on fruitless pursuits. Such women contrive to procure precious stones and metals of all kinds. . . . They do not give anyone a second to breathe with their incessant demands![44]

Goodness was often at the forefront of Nazarene missions as hospitals, clinics, and schools were erected around the world. These were all built upon the foundation of faith with the nature of Christ being visibly present in doing good and speaking to injustice. This has been a visible sign of who we are as a holiness people of God. We have understood the connection between goodness and justice, but when the two become disconnected, we have to reflect on whether we are continuing to grow as God's holy people.

44. Basil, Homily 7, "To the Rich," 4.47.

QUESTIONS FOR REFLECTION

1. What do the clothes that you wear say about you?

_____

_____

_____

2. What will it take for your spiritual life to burn with full combustion?

_____

_____

_____

3. How does your culture influence your movement toward God?

_____

_____

_____

4. Will you climb the mountain, and if so, what do you need to do to keep growing spiritually?

_____

_____

_____

5. What happens when someone can speak the language of holiness fluently but is wearing the wrong clothing?

_____

_____

_____

6. How would you share your own transformation story?

_____

_____

_____

7. In what acts of goodness have you participated?

_____

_____

_____

9

BLUE
Spiritual Formation, Part 2

Dany and Carla

The car stopped on the crowded street, near the top of a hill. Houses lined the road so that we couldn't see what was below. The district superintendent and the principal of the school greeted us and showed us the way to a set of stone stairs that would lead to the schoolyard at the bottom of a steep hill. As we climbed down in the direction of the school, we heard the drums beating and the children singing. This school was in the heart of Antananarivo, the capital city of Madagascar. For many years hundreds of street children had been ministered to through the school built in partnership with Nazarene Compassionate Ministries.

We were ushered around the building to view a new chapel, which had just been completed. We were there to dedicate the facility. Carla was asked to remove the drape from the dedication plaque and then to cut the ribbon. That was followed by a service of celebration with young people singing and dancing. Dany preached a dedication message and prayed a blessing over the new facility. To conclude the evening, we were to cut the huge cake that had been made for the celebration and then join everyone in enjoying the hospitality of our hosts. This church and school had been a place of transformation for hundreds of street children, many of whom were now leaders in the church.

It takes courage to keep growing spiritually and to press on toward knowledge. The use of this word is fascinating in Peter's context because the Roman world was obsessed with special hidden knowledge or *gnosis*. Society valued and esteemed those who may have had knowledge beyond what was commonly understood. This concept had crept into the church and resulted in a heresy known as Gnosticism. The problem with Gnosticism was that it was knowledge for the sake, or the good, of the individual and not of the community or society. Returning to Peter's epistle, when you clothe yourself in faith and are shaped by goodness, then knowledge will thrive for the benefit of all.

The world before us is changing rapidly. For many it no longer resembles the world into which we were born. As God's people, being shaped and formed on the journey, we are called to serve in this new reality. Try as we may, we want to be prepared for what lies ahead, but this is going to have to be a corporate enterprise. Only as we learn from one another and unite, clothed in God's garments, will we be able to face the future.

Frederick Buechner in *Telling the Truth* says, "People are prepared for everything except for the fact that beyond the darkness of their blindness there is a great light."[45] We may

45. Frederick Buechner, *Telling the Truth: The Gospel as Tragedy, Comedy, and Fairy Tale* (New York: HarperCollins, 1977).

feel that we are in a dark place. Far too much is beyond our understanding, but beyond our struggle there is a light that is greater than anything we can imagine. To reach the light, we have to continue the journey, but sometimes we don't feel that we have the energy to push forward. We become content to stay right where we are, even if it is in the darkness. Buechner warns us that we will miss out on what God has for us:

> They are prepared to go on breaking their backs plowing the same old field until the cows come home without seeing, until they stub their toes on it, that there is a treasure buried in that field rich enough to buy Texas. They are prepared for a God who strikes hard bargains but not for a God who gives as much for an hour's work as for a day's. They are prepared for a mustard-seed kingdom of God no bigger than the eye of a newt but not for the great banyan it becomes with birds in its branches singing Mozart.
>
> [We] are prepared for the potluck supper at [church] but not for the marriage supper of the Lamb, and when the bridegroom finally arrives at midnight with vine leaves in his hair, [we] turn up with [our] lamps to light him on his way all right only [we] have forgotten the oil to light them with and stand there with [our] big, bare, virginal feet glimmering faintly in the dark.[46]

This is the life of believers who stop following Jesus halfway up the mountain. They may make it part of the way, but then they fall into a routine that takes them nowhere. Outwardly, they look the part, testifying to entire sanctification and following all the rules of the *Manual*, while inwardly, they have stop growing. Practicing goodness has been rewarding, but by failing to continue on to knowledge, their spiritual growth has become stunted.

46. Buechner, *Telling the Truth*.

Knowledge is to be understood in relation to God. No one is to imagine that they have all knowledge and understanding, for that belongs to God alone. We are to have a bent toward learning, a hunger for more understanding, and a thirst for knowledge. With this mindset, we don't go into the world thinking that we have all the answers, but we go looking for treasure. In humility we approach new settings and cultures with a desire to learn. Michael Goheen says we are not to be like pearl merchants, but like treasure hunters: "Pearl merchants have something to give, whereas treasure hunters come empty-handed looking for the treasure already present in various cultures of the world."[47] To be clothed in knowledge is to live humbly in an ever-changing world, always willing to learn something new.

The journey had been arduous, starting early in the morning and going through security more times than one would care to recount. It included a stopover in Addis Ababa and a time of coffee and sharing with leaders whose stories of faith are straight out of the New Testament. We laughed, prayed, and praised God together before having to be whisked out the door and to the next airport. The small propeller plane rolled to the terminal and we were ushered out to find a seat. The flight was not long but when we landed, you could tell immediately that we were far from the modern city we had just left behind. In a four-wheel drive vehicle, we bounced over pocketed dirt roads through the heavy green forest. Finally, a town came into view, bustling with activity. This was the hub of life for many who were living in the numerous refugee camps in the surrounding territory. Thousands of South Sudanese had come to this place to find safety and rest from the violence they had experienced at home.

47. Michael W. Goheen, *Introducing Christian Mission Today: Scripture, History, and Issues* (Downers Grove, IL: InterVarsity Press, 2014), 285.

The missionaries did not go into the refugee camps as pearl salesmen, but looking for hidden treasures from God. What they discovered were camps filled with men, women, young people, and children, hungry to know more about Jesus. They told their stories and many began the journey of faith. Sunday morning we were taken to the local church where many people would gather for a special day of ordination. The missionaries had not only told the people about Jesus but also helped them to grow and to gain knowledge. There, within the walls of the refugee camps, schools had been established to help train pastors and leaders.

In the Old Testament, we find the familiar story of Daniel and his three friends, Shadrach, Meshach and Abednego. These young men had been intentionally raised to serve the Lord. Little did they know that their service would take place in a foreign land. Exiled, they had to learn how to survive in the midst of a new and unfamiliar context.

When life doesn't go according to plan, it's easy to make excuses. Why continue following Jesus up the mountain when things go wrong? Daniel and his three friends had been raised to lead God's people in Israel—or so they thought. Exile never became an excuse for these men and they refused to be deterred from the path to which they had been called. Selected by the Babylonians for leadership training, they took their responsibility seriously. Extremely self-disciplined, they were careful with their physical bodies as well as their minds. Taking advantage of the great knowledge they found in Babylon, they applied themselves and received an excellent education. Religious training and the study of the Torah had been a part of their childhood education, but now, to be the leaders that God wanted them to be, they applied themselves to the task of learning. They studied far beyond what they had learned back in Israel and became skilled in literature and wisdom.

It was to Daniel that God gave supernatural ability: He was to apply all that he had learned in the interpretation of visions and dreams. Everything that they did, all of their work, was to be done in humility and service before the Lord. As a result, these young men eventually became great leaders in the nation, respected for their wisdom—even though they were aliens! Somehow, they understood that they needed to be armed with all that was offered to them, even by way of a foreign king, and in this way they were able to navigate the uncharted waters of their world.

Education has always been a vital building block of the work of the church. Those who set out to establish missions in Eswatini believed that schools were a necessary outgrowth of missions. Even today, you can drive through the kingdom of Eswatini and see a sign for a Nazarene school every few kilometers. But has the attitude toward knowledge and education changed in recent years? Culture has made the world consumers and suddenly education is not necessarily for the greater good but has become a product to be purchased by the consumer. Instead of investing in education for the sake of the community, the consumer looks for the product that can be purchased at the cheapest price and with the least amount of effort. Let's call it "instant" education and/or gratification.

The problem with this plan is that in the long run, it won't produce the depth of leadership that we find in Daniel and his friends. For years they applied themselves to the study of the culture, literature, and scientific knowledge of the Babylonians. As a result, these four young men literally turned the tide of an entire nation of people toward God—and not only their people, but also the people of the foreign land in which they were living. This does not mean that everything always went their way. They encountered a lions' den and a very hot oven, but they maintained their integrity and stood on the truth they had come to know. They knew the Word of God, but they also knew the laws of the land and were clever enough to use them both for good.

The shortcuts of today will not provide us with the kinds of leaders that we need for the future. Our world is not becoming simpler; it's becoming more complex. For Christians to be able to navigate the major changes we are facing, we need those who will be willing to pay the price, both financially and in the investment of time, to learn all they can, and then apply those truths in leadership. While challenging, this type of education must become accessible to all of God's children. When we fail to provide pathways for all those capable to receive an education, we put limits on those who will be allowed to serve in positions of leadership. It may appear to be a daunting enterprise and yet God is calling some of his children to make a commitment; to pay the price to become the kind of influential and well-educated leader that God needs for the future. The world is in desperate need of a myriad of Christian voices that can speak into the complex issues of our day.

Let's return to that Sunday morning in Ethiopia. The young people gathered in the church, hundreds of them, all refugees from another land. There they listened as Dany shared the story of Daniel, Shadrach, Meshach, and Abednego. Riveted, they hung on every word as they listened to the challenge to have faith in God and practice goodness, but to also make sure they were prepared for what God may have in store for their future. Many were already taking advantage of every opportunity that was afforded them, even while living in a refugee camp.

After a short break, the ordination service began. Twenty-three individuals—sixteen women and seven men—came forward to be ordained, either as a deacon or elder in the church.

These individuals had already taken the time to study and be prepared for current and future ministry. Most of the ordinands were from the refugee camps, ministering among their fellow travelers who had also escaped from war at home. Knowing they might never return to their homeland, they were preparing for a new future, one in which their knowledge and faith in Jesus Christ would go with them. Whether they would be sent to Alaska, Texas, or Western Europe, they were now prepared to be missionaries, sharing the good news of Jesus all along the way. They had added to their faith, goodness and knowledge.

These sisters and brothers in Christ showed us the courage that is needed to continually be clothed in the virtues of Christlikeness. The apostle Peter knew that this wasn't the end of the journey and that there would be more robes to be worn. As the additional layers are added, the bride radiates with beauty.

Somehow the temptations of the flesh seem to transcend cultural barriers and geographic boundaries. Life in the kingdom of God calls for self-control, an ability to show restraint when facing the opportunity to indulge one's physical desires. Clothing oneself with self-control may require the setting of intentional boundaries, and these may need to be reset time and time again.

The apostle Paul often expressed his concerns about sexual immorality. The Roman world of the first century was filled with every kind of sexual activity imaginable. For those coming to Christ out of Roman society, the call to Christlikeness was deeply countercultural. False teachers were trying to entice new believers to give in to every physical desire, which often had negative consequences. Finally, after being led astray, they would become instruments of seduction themselves.[48]

48. Daniel Powers, *1 & 2 Peter/Jude: A Commentary in the Wesleyan Tradition*, *New Beacon Bible Commentary* (Kansas City: Beacon Hill Press of Kansas City, 2010).

The domino effect created by a lack of self-control is devastating, and much more so, in the church. The stories don't need to come from Africa or America or Europe, because they are written everywhere. The lack of self-control creates a web of pain and suffering, from the one who is abused, to the family of the abuser, and to the church members whose faith is shaken. The witness of the church is tarnished because the world knows that people who proclaim a message of holiness should be practicing self-control.

Temptations of the flesh are not only sexual in nature. There is a saying: "Americans live to eat while the rest of the world eats to live." Obesity has become a leading cause of poor health in more developed nations. The abundance and variety of foods available has become a temptation spread before people on the supermarket shelves and restaurant tables. Self-control is intentional self-denial for the sake of knowing Christ. When we take care of the physical bodies God has given us, we are better prepared to engage in ministry. When we intentionally deny ourselves food for a period of fasting, we draw closer to the Lord.

Closely tied to self-control is perseverance. We cannot simply practice self-control on one occasion and be finished, but the practice must become a part of life. Relationships also require perseverance. Dany, Anelie, and Carla had finished a long day of travel and had gone to dinner to talk about the events planned for the following day. Part of the conversation included a review of the meeting they had just completed.

As the evening wore on, it appeared that Dany was upset. Something had gone wrong in the conversation, and after perseverance, it was discovered that there was a cultural misunderstanding over something that had been said. One person perceived it in one way, while this had not been the intention of the other. When we come from different cultures and backgrounds at times we may think we are speaking the same language, but no one understands what is being said. For brothers and sisters in the faith to get along with one another, there must be perseverance, which is a commitment to continue pressing on, even when difficult. That evening the three of us pushed on with the conversation until we discovered the misunderstanding. Only by persevering, refusing to give up, were we able to clear up what had gone wrong. Through perseverance we continue the upward climb, and the bride's garments continue to be knit together uniting God's holy people.

As we are clothed in God's garments along the spiritual journey, a family resemblance begins to develop. Interestingly, that family resemblance transcends culture, race, ethnicity, and gender. The call to put on godliness is an attitude of respect toward the authority of God. This includes submission to the will of God, which influences our behavior toward others. Whether our brother in Christ is from Russia or Malawi, it doesn't matter; we will respect all of humanity because all are created in the image of God. This is why mutual affection is a natural outgrowth of our attitude toward God. The way that we act toward others bears witness to our walk with Christ. Brotherly love within the community of faith is a result of spiritual maturity and a life of holiness.

Jesus's desire was that the world would look upon the church in all her beauty and see how those within her walls loved one another. Jesus commanded his disciples, "Love one another. Just as I have loved you, you also should love one another. By this everyone will know that you are my disciples, if you have love for one another" (John 13:34-35, NRSV).

Interestingly, Jesus didn't say that they were only to love people who were just like them. He didn't tell them to minister among people of their own class and culture, but he sent them out into the whole world to share the good news of the kingdom of God. This is why Paul could declare, "There is no longer Jew or Greek, there is no longer slave or free, there is no longer male and female; for all of you are one in Christ Jesus. And if you belong to Christ, then you are Abraham's offspring, heirs according to the promise" (Galatians 3:28–29, NRSV). The upward call includes wearing God's beautiful robes of holiness. The spiritual life burns purely and the world looks on in amazement that people from every nation, race, and gender can be brought together as one in Christ Jesus.

Mutual affection, or brotherly love continually draws us toward the source of all holy love, Jesus. The pinnacle of the journey leads us to the pure unadulterated love. "See what love the Father has given us, that we should be called children of God; and that is what we are" (1 John 3:1, NRSV). The New International Version says that God has "lavished" this love on us. Out of God's overabundance of holy love, we are invited to become partakers of his divine nature. We are to become participants in God's holy love, falling deeper in love with our Lord day after day after day. No wonder the flame burns bright and pure, for there is no longer any corruption, for we are entirely in Christ.

We don't get to pick and choose the virtues, but they birth one after the other. This is the journey back up the mountain, following and participating in Christ, living a life energized by the presence of the Holy Spirit. Peter set this lofty journey before all believers, but it is not placed before us as an unattainable goal. This is God's invitation into a life of holiness that makes it possible for all to be "blameless and innocent, children of God without blemish in the midst of a crooked and perverse generation, in which you shine like stars in the world" (Philippians 2:15, NRSV).

As we mentioned before, the fall of the minister is devastating. The early church fathers said that if you were not continuing in your upward climb, you were actually losing ground in your spiritual life, going as far as to call the lack of spiritual growth a sin. We have witnessed the life of the busy pastor and church leader; the one who has put their own spiritual growth off to the side as they have helped others, only to fall themselves.

In Genesis 28:6–14 we find a rather obscure passage. It's the description of the garments that Aaron and his sons were to wear before the Lord. While it's a physical description of the garment, there is more to the story. The early church fathers saw in the description of the garment more than just the design of a piece of clothing, believing that God was speaking to the people about the virtues of those who serve in the priesthood. The colors that were selected for the ancient priestly garments were intentionally conspicuous so the priest would stand out, understanding that there was a standard for service before God greater than that of the ordinary person. This clothing foreshadowed the life of holiness. There is a message here for those who are called to serve as elders and deacons in the church. Personal participation in Christ is to be a roadmap for those under the care of a minister. Therefore, there must be great sensitivity to the upward call, and the minister's life is to be adorned with the clothing of Christ.

We came to the end of the day in Nigeria. It had been a great celebration of ordination as we sang and danced while worshipping the Lord, all dressed in clothing made from the same fabric. This fabric was imprinted with the seal of the Church of the Nazarene. We had to go straight from the service to the airport to catch our plane out to Lagos. Anelie and Carla had no time to change their clothes and arrived at the airport adorned in dresses that advertised our participation in the Church of the Nazarene. The check-in agent, luggage handlers, and security guards all commented on our beautiful dresses. There was no doubt that we were clothed as messengers of the Church of the Nazarene.

When we are clothed in the character of Christ, wearing every garment that is prepared for the bride, we become living ambassadors of Jesus. It's God's intention that the world would look with awe at the church and the beauty of her garments, made up not only of many layers but also of varied colors, and held together by the golden thread of doctrine—holiness.

QUESTIONS FOR REFLECTION

1. What new knowledge have you gained lately? What practices do you have in your life to keep learning?

_____

_____

2. Why is self-control vital to the Christian life?

_____

_____

3. How does our spiritual growth affect the ways in which we engage with brothers and sisters of differing ethnicities or cultures?

_____

_____

4. What is something practical you can do to participate in a culture that is different from yours?

_____

_____

5. How does mutual affection become a witness to the presence of Christ?

_____

_____

10

MUSIC IS A COLOR

Let's Sing a New Song

Dany and Carla

"One thing I asked of the LORD, that will I seek after: to live in the house of the LORD all the days of my life, to behold the beauty of the LORD, and to inquire in his temple."

—*Psalm 27:4, NRSV*

I, Dany, love music, and it has been a shaping force in my life. A friend of mine once said that music decorates time, for music is indeed a part of life, and in many cultures, it even gives rhythm to life. Music is a passion I inherited from my father, and African drums, reggae, and jazz music are my favorites. African drums are first of all about rhythm; "there is no movement without rhythm," for it is the balance of everyday life, and it is about the real stories of life.[49] In *The Spirituals and the Blues*, James Cone masterfully captures the deep connection between Africans and African Americans: "Since 'the chief concern of African music was to recite the history of the people.' Therefore, when Africans were brought to America, they carried with them the art of storytelling through music."[50]

The art of storytelling through music is still commonly practiced among story-centric people around the world and is also present in key moments in the Bible when we encounter the people of God. In the Old Testament, we find a passage in Exodus 15, which is sometimes called the Song of Moses. Said to have been composed by Moses's sister, Miriam, this song is a beautiful example of the art of storytelling through music. In the song, the acts of the Almighty God are recounted to the people, and the lyrics become the essence of worship, recounting who God is, what he has done, and affirming his promises: "Who is like you, O LORD, among the gods? Who is like you, majestic in holiness, awesome in splendor, doing wonders? You stretched out your right hand, the earth swallowed them" (Exodus 15:11–12, NRSV).

In the New Testament, we find another beautiful song. Mary, the mother of our Lord Jesus, tells the great deeds of the Almighty God in one of the four songs of the infancy narrative: "My soul magnifies the Lord, and my spirit rejoices in God my Savior . . . for the Mighty One has done great things for me, and holy is his name" (Luke 1:46, 49, NRSV). God invites each of us to develop the practice of simply worshipping through storytelling, just like Miriam and Mary did. We are to sing

49. The Rhythm Project and A Moving Company, "FOLI (there is no movement without rhythm) original version by Thomas Roebers and Floris Leeuwenberg," https://www.youtube.com/watch?v=lVPLIuBy9CY&list=PL86jqfAltQu3mP0NiTWSzNMXOpm3JfimF.

50. James H. Cone, *The Spirituals and the Blues* (Maryknoll, NY: Orbis Books), 232.

our own song, with our own words, from our own experience, telling the majestic acts of God in our everyday life. While this storytelling is done in our own language, the Spirit unites us together into one body. This may be what William Wadé Harris[51] was referring to when he emphatically said: "God has no favorite songs! I have never been to heaven, so I cannot tell you what kind of music is sung in God's royal village. But know this, that God has no personal favorite songs. He hears all that we say in whatever language. It is sufficient for us to offer hymns of praise to him with our own music and in our own language for him to understand."[52]

Or it may be what Nigerian author Chinua Achebe described in his classic *Things Fall Apart* when the young Ikemefuna heard a Christian hymn for the first time and the lyrics were interpreted in his heart language: "He felt a relief within as the hymn poured into his parched soul. The words of the hymn were like the drops of frozen rain melting on the dry palate of the panting earth."[53]

Finally, it may be the vision of John in Revelation: "After this I looked, and there before me was a great multitude that no one could count, from every nation, tribe, people and language, standing before the throne and before the Lamb" (Revelation 7:9). The focus here is not on the number nor the diversity nor the inclusiveness, but on the uniqueness ("every") and the equality (all "standing"). Everyone present was in the same position of readiness, of expectation, and of reverent worship in

51. William W. Harris (c. 1860–1929) was a Liberian Grebo evangelist who preached in Liberia, Côte d'Ivoire, and Ghana. He has been described as the "most extraordinary one-man evangelical crusade that Africa has ever known."

52. Roberta King, N. J. Kidula, J. R. Krabill, and T. A. Oduro, *Music in the Life of the African Church* (Baylor, TX: Baylor University Press, 2008), 64–65.

53. Chinua Achebe, *The African Trilogy* (New York: Penguin Publishing Group, 2017), 12.

their own uniqueness, their own story, and their own identity. All are standing in their identity as children, and as coheirs with the Lord Jesus Christ.

What about jazz? Jazz is a musical genre born in the United States among the African American people of New Orleans. Some say it started at the place called "Congo Square." This was the space in New Orleans where black slaves were allowed to gather one day a week and sing, dance, and fellowship. The slaves from different nations would take their turn in the square, teaching the traditional dances and music to their neighbors and the next generation. This square became fertile ground for the storytelling and the retention of their African culture through music, and out of this developed jazz.

When I talk about jazz, I am referring first of all to its African origins. Jazz was birthed among an oppressed people who expressed the richness of their soul through rhythms and generosity, with openness and ingenuity that resulted in innovation and integration of the surrounding cultures into the music. I like jazz because of its universality and adaptability as a music that has been adopted and played by cultures around the world without losing uniqueness. It is in many ways similar to Christ in the cultures around the world. Christ is expressed in different ways, but the essence of his message and person are never lost. As missiologist Lamin Sanneh put it, "Christianity was a religion for all seasons, fit for all humanity. Whatever its core was, it was not in any one time, in any one place, or in any one language."[54]

When we begin to hear music playing quietly in the distance, it becomes an overture, and we want to draw near. In the same way, the gospel is first and foremost an invitation,

54. Lamin Sanneh, *Disciples of All Nations: Pillars of World Christianity* (Oxford: Oxford University Press, 2008), 14.

for the good news about Jesus is a message of hospitality, a story to be shared with everyone. Peter confessed before a crowd of gentiles: "Truly I understand that God shows no partiality, but in every nation anyone who fears him and does what is right is acceptable to him" (Acts 10:34–35, ESV). God the Father sees all men and women who fear him and are of goodwill. We don't always have the same vision as God, and with our eyes we tend to identify people through race, gender, and social status. The power of the gospel can make the scales fall from our religious eyes and give us new insight into the masses of children and friends who are running away from the Father.

As we've seen, the essence of worship is to recount who God is and what he has done and affirm his promises. While this is true, worship is also about entering God's heart of hospitality. When this is the case, we are urged to bring our brothers and sisters who are still far away to the Father's house. The music of worship is to be a song of hospitality, and this is God's mission to the world.

A few months ago, a French Christian song I had not heard for forty years came to my mind. In the song, the singer talked about searching for his friends, including those who were "living in the night" or separated from God. Usually, we think the gospel is about going out to seek those who are lost, and we tend to label them as pagans. We are like the apostle Peter, who considered Cornelius a pagan—a gentile, one who should not have known anything about God. However, God saw Cornelius as one of his children, one who had become separated from the Father. Peter had to learn a lesson as God opened his eyes to embrace that which he had called "unclean" for his entire life. For far too long we've put labels on "others" and have not imagined them as children, separated from their Father. We are called to go to our brothers and sisters and bring them into reconciliation with our common Father.

The song also speaks to us from the life of the writer, himself. The author of this song is John Littleton, an African American son of a Baptist pastor and farmer, who was born on a plantation in Louisiana in 1930. Later in life, he traveled to France during his military service and married a French woman. He lived the rest of his life in France, dying in the city of Reims in 1998. He became known as the most famous French gospel singer of his generation, selling millions of recordings. In John Littleton, we see the beautiful example of the coat of many colors, where someone from another culture and race, with a different religious tradition entered a different world and became a part of the community. He then transcended his host culture to produce a message of hope and peace that spoke to the generation of his time.

The coat of many colors is not the good news in and of itself, but it is the result of the work the good news does in our hearts and lives. Just as music knows no cultural borders, so we are to live as if music were a color. It's a beautiful space that touches our hearts, minds, and souls; out of it flows love for God and for our brothers and sisters. In some ways, we would like to just stay in this place and enjoy the music. In John's gospel we read, "So when the Samaritans came to him, they urged him to stay with them, and he stayed two days" (John 4:40). He stayed two days, but then he had to keep moving, for he was on a mission.

We are to join Jesus on this mission, but we must be ready. There is a need to be intentional about diversity, honoring the beautiful colors in our midst, but we cannot pander to culture. Music is indeed a color, but it is everyone's choice to decide which song fits the best, and from time to time that song changes. The robe is being sewn together, but you are now called to participate in the pattern for the future. Just like the messianic view of the church found in Psalm 45, we are to be prepared in our many-colored robes, entering the presence of the king with joy and gladness. The African author Cheikh Hamidou Kane challenges us to think about the future: "We have not had the same past, but—unquestionably—we shall have the same future. The era of individual destinies is over. Thus the end of the world has really arrived for each of us, for none can live any longer taking thought only for self-preservation."[55]

The flight to Windhoek was fewer than two hours, but this was yet another country to be explored. Namibia was to be a place of contrasts, where the church members were from several different cultures. The urban church had planted new suburban churches but had then reached out to the ethnic group area of the north. The word of the Lord had spread and the assembly saw a unique group of people—black, white, colored, urban and educated, rural and illiterate—all gathered together as a community of faith.

The time came for elections to be held but there weren't enough ballots for all the delegates present and this created frustration. The secretary left the assembly to find a copier to make more ballots, but something needed to be done to fill the time and help cut through the tension in the room. Dany jumped to the platform and grabbed a microphone, asking the people to follow him. He sang a line of a song—they echoed back. Then he sang another line—they echoed. The musicians ran to the platform and joined in—the keyboardist trying to find the right key and the drummer beginning to pick up the beat.

55. Quoted in Ela, *My Faith*, 12.

Pretty soon everyone had gotten up and joined the music. A couple of people stepped into the aisle and began to dance toward the front of the sanctuary. Others joined in as their faces beamed with joy. People in Western clothing and others dressed in traditional garb followed one another around the sanctuary singing praises to God. Suddenly, all the tension was gone, and we were one in Christ.

And we were one in Christ!

QUESTION FOR REFLECTION

Where do you go from here? If we are to be God's holy people we cannot stay the same. What truths do you take from this book to make change in your own life?

_____

_____

_____

BIBLIOGRAPHY

Achebe, Chinua. *The African Trilogy*. New York: Penguin Publishing Group, 2017.

Augustine, "Sermons 63.1–3." Trans. R. G. MacMullen. From *Nicene and Post-Nicene Fathers*, First Series, Vol. 6. Ed. Philip Schaff. Buffalo, NY: Christian Literature Publishing Co., 1888. Rev. and ed. for New Advent by Kevin Knight. http://www.newadvent.org/fathers/160363.htm.

Aulen, Gustaf. *Christus Victor* Austin, TX: Wise Path Books, 2016.

Basil of Caesarea. *Homilia(e)* (PG 29:209-494; 31:163-618, 1429-1514). Trans. Agnes Clare Way, *The Fathers of the Church: Basil of Caesarea, Exegetical Homilies*, Vol. 56, ed. Joseph Deferrari. Washington, DC: The Catholic University of America Press, 1963.

Basset, Paul M. *Holiness Teaching: New Testament Times to Wesley.* 3 vols. *Great Holiness Classics*. Kansas City: Beacon Hill Press of Kansas City, 1997.

Biko, Steve. *I Write What I Like: A Selection of His Writings.* Johannesburg: Heinemann Publishers, 1978.

Brower, Kent. *Mark: A Commentary in the Wesleyan Tradition, New Beacon Bible Commentary.* Kansas City: Beacon Hill Press of Kansas City, 2012.

Brown, Brené. *Dare to Lead.* New York: Random House Publishing Group, 2018.

Buechner, Frederick. *Telling the Truth: The Gospel as Tragedy, Comedy, and Fairy Tale.* New York: HarperCollins, 1977.

Cone, James H. *The Spirituals and the Blues: An Interpretation.* Maryknoll, NY: Orbis Books, 1992.

Ela, Jean-Marc. *My faith as an African.* Eugene, OR: Wipf and Stock Publishers, 1988.

Fanon, Frantz. *Black Skin, White Masks.* New York: Grove Press, 1967.

Flemming, Dean E. *Philippians: A Commentary in the Wesleyan Tradition, New Beacon Bible Commentary.* Kansas City: Beacon Hill Press of Kansas City, 2009.

Geisler, Norman. L. *I Don't Have Enough Faith to Be an Atheist.* Wheaton, IL: Crossway Publishers, 2007.

Girvin, Ernest Alexander. *Phineas F. Bresee: A Prince in Israel, a Biography.* Kansas City: Pentecostal Nazarene Publishing House, 1916.

Goheen, Michael W. *Introducing Christian Mission Today: Scripture, History, and Issues.* Downers Grove, IL: InterVarsity Press, 2014.

Greathouse, William H. "Sanctification and the *Christus Victor* Motif," *Africa Speaks: An Anthology of the Africa Nazarene Theology Conference 2003.* South Africa: Africa Nazarene Publications, 2004.

Gregory of Nyssa. *De Perfectione* (*On Perfection*) (DP) (PG 46:249). Gregorii Nysseni opera, ed. Werner Jaeger, with others, 8:1. Leiden, The Netherlands: Brill, 1963. Trans. Virginia Callahan in *St. Gregory Ascetical Works, Fathers of the Church*, Vol. 58. Washington, DC: Catholic University of America Press, 1999.

———. *In Canticum Canticorum* (*Commentary on the Canticle*) (CC) (PG 44:756–1120). Gregorii Nysseni opera, ed. H. Langerbeck, vol. 6. Leiden, The Netherlands: Brill, 1960. In Daniélou, Jean. *From Glory to Glory: Texts from the Gregory of Nyssa's Mystical Writings*. Trans. Herbert Musurillo. Crestwood, NY: St. Vladimir's Press, 2001.

King, Roberta Rose, Jean Ngoya Kidula, James R. Krabill, and Thomas Oduro. *Music in the Life of the African Church*. Baylor, TX: Baylor University Press, 2008.

Kuma, Afua. *Jesus of the Deep Forest: Prayers and Praises of Afua Kuma*. Accra, Ghana: Asempa Publishers, 1981.

Lewis, C. S. *The Great Divorce*. New York: Macmillan, 1946.

Powers, Daniel. *1 & 2 Peter/Jude: A Commentary in the Wesleyan Tradition. Beacon Bible Commentary.* Kansas City: Beacon Hill Press of Kansas City, 2010.

Sanders, J. Oswald. *The Incomparable Christ*. Chicago: Moody Publishers, 1952.

Sanneh, Lamin O. *Disciples of All Nations: Pillars of World Christianity*. Oxford: Oxford University Press, 2008.

Snow, Robert S. and Arseny Ermakov. *Matthew: A Commentary in the Wesleyan Tradition, New Beacon Bible Commentary*. Kansas City: The Foundry Publishing, 2019.

Sunberg, Carla D. *The Cappadocian Mothers: Deification Exemplified in the Writings of Basil, Gregory, and Gregory*. Eugene, OR: Pickwick Publications, 2018.

Toffler, Alvin. *Future Shock*. New York: Bantam Books, 1970.

Wilken, Robert Louis. *The Spirit of Early Christian Thought: Seeking the Face of God*. New Haven, CT: Yale University Press, 2003.